I STILL WARM THE TEAPOT

Humorous, critical and reflective pieces of writing

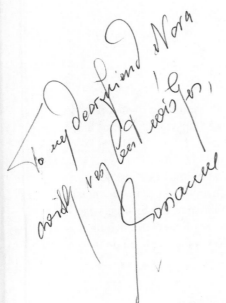

Marianne MacKinnon

M Books

First published in 2011 by
MM Books
(formerly Hillcrest Books)
6 Hog Green
Elham
Kent CT4 6TU

ISBN 978-0-9521447-3-1

Also by Marianne MacKinnon:

The Naked Years

The Alien Years

The Deluge

The Quarry

Reflections

A Slow Boat to Hong Kong

German-born **Marianne MacKinnon** was educated at Potsdam, Oxford and at Strathclyde University. At the end of the Second World War she worked for the US and British Military Government in Germany, trained as a nurse in England, and worked in Italy and Spain. In 1961 she accompanied her husband, a British Intelligence Officer, on his posting to Hong Kong, working variously as a translator, Court Interpreter and VIP hostess while bringing up their three young children. In more recent years she concentrated on her writing, publishing an award-winning memoir of her life under Hitler and then under military occupation *(The Naked Years)*. A sequel *(The Alien Years)* recalls her experiences in post-war England, which she followed up with two critically-acclaimed novels, *The Deluge* and *The Quarry*. A memoir of her time in Hong Kong, *A Slow Boat to Hong Kong*, is now available in paperback. Today she lives in East Kent, where she teaches creative writing.

CONTENTS

Like as the waves make towards the pebbled shore
So do our minutes hasten to their end;
Each changing place with that which goes before
In sequent toil all forwards do contend.

Shakespeare, Sonnet 60

FOREWORD

My reflections on life and death, God and religion, the quality of life, changes in our society, traditional and modern values, and on other matters close to my heart which begged to be addressed, were often triggered off by a trivial daily event, a person's remark or attitude or the tenor of a newspaper article. They always led to thoughts on larger issues and sometimes to journeys into the past. At the time of writing I did not have publication in mind. Free of the criteria which publishers and reading trends nowadays impose, I filled a void in my life by divesting myself of thoughts which have been waiting for some time to be analysed, thought through, formulated and put down on paper. In this, my love for the written word has helped me, as did an inner urge to give my views some philosophical latitude.

At the risk of being credited by some with a virile imagination, by others with old lady-ish sentiments, I admit that there have been times when I felt some higher inspirational authority, perhaps a divine spirit, had put a pen into my hand. Sentences then flowed on paper like fine hourglass sand, and without my first having to examine the validity of a theme, or structure a paragraph. Sometimes I felt a strong sense behind it, sometimes I felt I was being dictated to. Yet I am no theologian, and in the face of the senseless ongoing carnage and human suffering in the world, I cannot call myself an unswerving believer. Nor do I have a university degree in any of the subjects I am writing about. My life alone provided me with a higher degree of learning, as did years of research at home and abroad. Writing skill, though it surfaced and developed at a later stage of my life, enables me to put into words my conclusions about what I have experienced in the past, and about what I am seeing, reading and living through today. In my essays I am not only presenting myself as a backroom philosopher and artless critic, but I am taking the lid off my inner feelings and convictions.

I STILL WARM MY TEAPOT shall be my legacy.

For my sons

I WAS A BERLINER

Much has been written over the years about the resurgence of Berlin as the capital of a country that rose like a Phoenix from the ashes of World War II. Once West Germany had been reunited with its eastern territory, to form the *Bundesrepublik*, Parliament made the spectacularly-rebuilt Berlin *Reichstag* its home. Ministries relocated, former Nazi buildings which survived the war were refurbished, and new executive apartment blocks were built to accommodate the army of government officials. Many West German and foreign companies soon re-sited their offices to the city, and investors and entrepreneurs were drawn to a new playing field like bees to nectar. Berlin, a *Weldstadt* once again, has since been staging international conferences and fairs; it attracts top-grade musicians, conductors, opera singers and stars from the world of film, theatre and dance. On the downside, and like any major city nowadays, it is equally a haven for illegal immigrants and criminal elements, many of whom managed to establish themselves in the wake of the *Mauerfall* and due to lenient government asylum policies.

The Wall, the concrete monstrosity which, together with the DDR's notorious death-strips, once symbolised the political chasm between East and West, relegated West Berlin for decades to a democratic island in a Red Sea. My family and I were sailing to Hong Kong in July 1961 when we heard over the ship's radio that by order of the East German (communist) government, a fortified wall had been built overnight along the eastern sector of Berlin and the length of the border between East and West Germany. It was a desperate measure to try and stop the exodus of skilled workers, which threatened to drain the DDR's economy. As a result, the country's remaining citizens found themselves 'imprisoned' for decades.

Once before the Wall went up, and before I got married to a member of the British Security Forces stationed in the

1

British Sector of Berlin, I visited its eastern sector. I remember the drabness of the new Soviet-style blocks of flats, the skeletons or shell-mutilated façades of grand buildings dating back to Kaiser's time. I remember the scarcity of goods in the shops and the many propaganda posters and portraits of Party leaders. And I clearly recall my sense of unease when I passed a member of the feared East German police.

I was living in Scotland when the news about the fall of the Wall broke. Surely, everybody who watched that event on television that night was moved by the euphoria of East Germans stepping into a new-found freedom, and by the welcome they received from Berliners and at other border openings. Yet, due to the multilateral problems created by the Reunification, jubilation soon turned to disappointment, and in West Berliners and West Germans burdened by *Wiedervereinigung* tax - into resentment. Not surprisingly so, for the economic setbacks soon proved too massive, the disparity between the eastern and western mentality, and between a capitalist and once communist-ruled society, too blatant, for the Bonn government to find a painless, magic solution.

In *The Quarry* I describe my impressions during my first visit to East Berlin and its DDR hinterland shortly after the dismantling of the Wall. I saw with my own eyes how a 'Big-Brother-is-watching-you' attitude had been ingrained in people. I saw the result of agricultural mismanagement, total environmental disregard and urban neglect.

Reunification is history now. East Germany and Berlin now form an essential part of the German Federal Republic. Yet sadly, while Berlin is a much-visited and highly-praised tourist destination again, it no longer welcomes me. It now makes me feel like a stranger, an outsider who has developed a love-hate relationship. Yet I was born there. In the mid-Twenties. And although I have been living in Britain or within British ex-pat communities abroad for well over fifty years, I have always kept a metaphorical suitcase in the city, a dichotomy which is based on what I nostalgically remember of my birthplace and its culture as a child and young woman, and what I see now as the new face of Berlin - features that are no longer compatible with those memories.

The history of the city throughout the centuries makes chilling reading. Due to its exposed geographical position, it was often at the mercy of foreign armies, was razed and looted, its people slaughtered or oppressed by various 'governing' Princes.

The Wilhelminian era presented to the world a brilliant feat of architecture, road building and technology together with a booming trade and commerce. This cosy picture, however, conflicted all too sharply with the dire poverty of Berliners who lived in the dark, damp *Hinterhof* tenements or in cellars. Behind that façade were the doss houses, long queues at the soup kitchens and the mute despair of millions of unemployed. At the time, Berlin was the most densely populated city in Europe, a melting pot of nineteenth century immigrants. Over the years it attracted people from all over the world, many of whom brought their technical know-how, financial expertise or artistic talents to the capital.

While the Holocaust made a shameful, non-obliterable blot on the country's historic landscape, Hitler's expansionist strategies - born out of his obsessive urge to erase the ill-fitting conditions of the Treaty of Versailles - progressed to World War II and Germany's final defeat. In Berlin, following years of hunger, rubble-clearing, foreign occupation and political isolation, it was mainly due to the valiant efforts of its citizens and foreign aid, that the city got back on its feet again. Since the Wall came down, it has enjoyed a radical face lift. Now that it bears capital status, it is bigger, brighter and boldly metropolitan. However, it is no longer the city in which I feel at home.

My image of the city is one in which poets and writers, architects, painters and stars of stage and screen left their mark. It is the Berlin of Heinrich Zille, who in his drawings set the city's beauty against its deprivations and moral decay, just as George Grosz virulently portrayed Berlin's bourgeoisie, German militarism and capitalist exploitation in his paintings, and Käthe Kollwitz tried to stir the conscience of the rich. It is also the Berlin of the painter Emil Nolde, the sculptor Georg Kolbe, the architects Schinkel, Schlüter, Walter Gropius, Knobelsdorff, Mies van der Rohe and the Bauhaus School. It is the city in which composers Kurt Weill and Paul Hindemith worked, as did the playwright Bertolt Brecht and the satirist Kurt Tucholsky. It is a city of artists, some of whom I came to know in my youth. Wilhelm Furtwängler, the famous conductor, is one of them. I am eternally grateful to my grandmother and mother to have taken me to the Philharmonic concerts at an early age, so that Furtwängler conducting Beethoven and Brahms symphonies cultivated my love for classical music. I also recall many of the most prominent film stars of the time, such as Heinrich George, Emil Jannings, and Adolf Wohlbrück, not forgetting such darlings of cinema-goers as Victor de Kowa, Hans Albers, Hildegard Knef, Heinz Rühmann, Willy Fritsch, Will Quadflieg, Marika Röck and many others who with their escapist films made the war years, and particularly the first grim post-war ones, bearable for Berliners.

I still feel privileged to have witnessed some highlights in the world of pre-war and war-time entertainment. High on the list are some brilliant variety shows in the Skala or Wintergarten with star-studded international casts. So are my first opera, Hänsel and Gretel, in the Deutsche Staatsoper Unter den Linden, a Furtwängler-conducted performance of the 'Meistersingers', and a grand production of Goethe's Faust II in the Schillertheater, which many critics saw as a *Sternenstunde*, a highlight of German theatre. And how can I ever forget the war-time performance of the Magic Flute, staged by the bombed-out Staatsoper ensemble in the Admiralspalast, in which Elizabeth Schwartzkopf sang the Queen of the Night? Like other opera lovers, the evening transported me into a magical, peaceful world, before I stepped out into the frosty night, still feeling dazed with the beauty of the music, and not wanting to realise that we were only an hour or less away from the harsh reality of the wailing sirens, the sight of the silver-toned bellies of American bombers and the fireworks of German flak batteries.

In the weeks before Christmas my thoughts often return to the Weihnachtsmarkt on the Lustgarten Square, to which my father would take me in the early Thirties. In the hard winters, which used to be the rule at the time, the snow would crunch under my boots, and my cheeks be aglow with the frost. The seasonal bouquet of cinnamon cookies, pine and candle wax, sugar-roasted almonds and candied apples on sticks would lap waves of happiness around me. Tinsel, wooden carved angels, gingerbread manikins, the voices of carol singers and briefly, a dusting of snow or the tolling of the Dom bells, completed this set-piece of Christmas-land.

My father also took me for strolls along Unter den Linden, the broad avenue east of the Brandenburg Gate. Lined by miles of lime trees, it was bordered by elegant shops, cafés and restaurants. My father might call on his tailor or buy a new hat, before treating me to lunch at his club, where amid gilt, red plush and chandelier splendour he ended up shooting a few billiard balls under the admiring eyes of his daughter.

Other cameos of my Berlin years spring to mind: sipping cream-laced hot chocolate at the famous Hotel Adlon, where my father used to entertain his company's clients for lunch or dinner; the luxury Hotel Fürstenhof, where I stayed overnight with my mother and her new husband, shortly before it was totally destroyed by a bomb. And every time I pass the part-ruin of the Kaiser Wilhelm Memorial Church, I am reminded of a yellowed photograph which shows my mother and father standing on the steps of the church after their wedding ceremony.

In *The Naked Years* I recall the Berlin Olympics in 1936, when in the flag-lined Unter den Linden my father and I had to thread our way through the throng of people and the medley of foreign languages. I also described my emotions when, sitting by my father's side, I watched the main athletic events, among them Jessie Owens' world record long jump and sprint.

During the floor-lit Gala Show and Youth Pageant, I danced with other white-clad schoolgirls on the Stadium's lush green oval to Rossini tunes, keenly watched by Hitler and his entourage; I listened with something akin to religious exultation to the jubilant strains of Beethoven's Ninth Symphony Chorus and the national anthem, during which spears of light were arching high over the bowl, to form a silver dome. For me, the ten year-old, who knew as yet nothing about the downside of National Socialism, and who, given a paper swastika flag, would cheerfully wave it at passing marching columns, my experiences during the Olympic Games are part of that short childhood which I spent with my parents. As such they are full of memorable, easily accessible details.

The Kurfürstendamm, which since the beginning of the twentieth century has also undergone some historic changes, is another landscape of which I have preserved lasting memories. I recall the famous 'Damm' as a child when, dressed in my Sunday clothes, my parents took me for a stroll down the boulevard. My father, always a smart dresser with a preference for dove grey felt hats, galoshes and suede gloves, carried himself like a man who knew his own worth. My mother was no less elegantly attired, and like other middle-class ladies would not be seen without a hat and gloves.

More than once our outing would end with a visit to Café Schilling, which dated back to the turn of the century. Here, crystal chandeliers, gilt mirrors, marble-topped tables and red plush upholstery attracted a select clientele which conducted their tea or coffee rites commensurate with the sophistication of the establishment. Into this nirvana of cream cakes and subdued chatter, I would tiptoe with the awe of my age, soon to forget everything around me over a Nusstörtchen[1].

More images of the Ku-Damm are taking shape: just before Goebbels declared 'total war', and all the theatres, dance cafés and bars had to close, I danced with a dashing young officer at the Café Wien. For the length of the romantic afternoon *Tanz-Tee*, from which neither the ersatz lemonade nor the frugal cake quality distracted, I forgot my homework, my poor marks in maths and physics, and whatever was waiting for me at the end of my schooldays.

Not long afterwards the face of the Kurfürstendamm changed, and by the end of the war most of its shops, cafés, cinemas and restaurants had fallen victim to Allied bombs. There were gaping holes, gutted buildings and shell-vandalised façades, and over the mounds of bricks and mortar dust there hung the nauseating smell of decomposing bodies. All the trees which had once added to the boulevard's rambling pleasure had gone, having been hacked down for firewood.

With the arrival of American troops, the Damm saw desperate women prostituting themselves for a packet of Camels or tin of corned beef, while the sight of haggard-looking men in tattered uniforms or on crutches, black market dealers and brigades of brick-clearing women further imparted an air of human wretchedness.

In the Fifties the Kurfürstendamm went through a gradual renaissance, but with most of its nineteenth century architectural features gone, and trashy shops opening up beside the first international high-fashion ventures and nocturnal haunts, its pre-war ambience had gone for good.

---

[1] Small, iced, cream-filled hazelnut cake

It was the time when friends took me to the Oasis, a Russian night club frequented by Russian émigrés. Here, the *borsch* was reputed to be the finest outside Russia. A three-man band played the balalaika, sang 'Kalinka' and accompanied the dancers' boots, which stamped and whirled to the rhythms of Mother Russia's music. (I believe the Oasis disappeared at the height of the Cold War, most likely as soon as the Wall went up.)

When I visited Berlin shortly after the fall of the Wall, I was witness to the Damm's resurgence as a strip for the pleasure-hungry. Over the years, my impressions were further enhanced by the various reportages of British newspaper columnists and travel writers.

Now that Berlin is the home of the German Parliament, the boulevard has lost its sex-crazy image which once gave the city the label of 'Sin City'. While cabaret shows might still try to mimic the aura of the Twenties with their satiric and decadent art form, and while Sally Bowles' Berlin seems to be saying once again 'Willkommen', 'Bienvenue', 'Welcome', the Kurfürstendamm no longer offers eroticism, transvestite and freak sex shows on a liberal plate. Now, the seedier night-haunts, which cater for those in search of titillating or gritty entertainment, have moved to the eastern parts of the city which is now reputed to be the main hang-out for former Kurfürstendamm prostitutes since they left the morally-cleaned up boulevard for more tolerant and profitable pastures.

Berlin may stun the visitor with the international flair of the city restaurants. Gone is its beer, pig's trotter and sauerkraut image. On the 'Damm's' favourite strolling mile, every palate is seemingly catered for. Smart gourmet restaurants vie for custom with cosy old-time pubs, and with eating places offering everything from hearty German dishes and bockwurst snacks to Peking duck, kebabs, Mexican curries, *Smörgåsbord*, pasta meals, vegetarian greens and American T-bone steaks. In roadside cafés, which in cold weather boast heated verandas, Berliners and visitors to the city alike are watching the crowds passing by - the constant flow of shoppers, group travellers, young lovers, punks, backpackers, dark-suited gentlemen with leather briefcases, young women in trendy clothes and ladies in understated designer creations. As in many western cities, the Damm is also the resort of pavement vendors, street musicians and commercial evangelists. Alas, like the forecourt of the Memorial Church, it is also the favourite hang-out for punks, drug peddlers and vagrants, not forgetting the loitering gangs of East Europeans and North African migrants, professional idlers and misfits of society. It is, however, this human tableau of the Ku-Damm which forms a special attraction for people watching the parade from a roadside seat over a coffee or a beer. It has the same magnetism for those who, like myself, are still nurturing earlier images of the boulevard, and who cannot help comparing its present aura, bustle and human *melée* with their own yellowed memories.

Berlin may feel justly proud of the regeneration of its eastern areas, its new political status, cultural rebirth and grand planning concepts. However, I realise with a touch of sadness that the city of my birth, childhood and young womanhood has gone for good.

So has the house in which I lived with my parents before they got divorced in thirty-six, which was completely gutted by bombs. Rebuilt after the war, albeit without balconies, fine stucco work and generous-sized windows, it looks like a travesty of the one I once knew.

From among many pavements which I walked with my young children, giant weeds are now sprouting, and the young roadside trees of the Seventies now provide ample shade for passers-by. My grandmother's house, restored to its former glory after a raging war-time fire, now houses doctors' surgeries on every floor. The red letterbox, to which I was often sent to post letters, has been painted steel blue. And there

9

is The Tree. Whenever my grandmother and I were passing this tree in a Zehlendorf suburban garden, she would heave a deep sigh and point her finger at the tree, on which her private banker had hanged himself following the Wall Street Crash in twenty-nine, and having taken her own and other people's substantial investments with him. The Tree is no more. Perhaps the owner of the property had it felled, to oust the banker's ghost.

And gone is the British Officers' Club, where from the late Sixties my family and I swam or played tennis; where my husband and I often dined in style or danced the night away to the music of an old-fashioned band. Gone, too, are the NAAFI building and Civilian Messes. Only fading memories remain.

I now need a street map to find my way around some parts of the city, in which new landmarks have been created to form the eastern backbone of the capital. During previous visits to Berlin I was always looking for something that was no longer there. However, with something akin to jubilation, I found one signpost of my childhood still existing: a three-inch wide hole in between the mosaic stone pavement which adjoins the grassed forecourt of the Nathanael Church in Friedenau - the freak cavity into which my young friend, Eduard, and I used to roll our coloured marbles in the early Thirties. It is a miracle how it survived the bombing and the post-war roadworks around it. Perhaps it is a reminder that while everything in life is in a constant flux and subject to change, the small and seemingly insignificant things often have a greater chance of survival.

Berlin, it is said, always lures back those who have turned their back on it. Its history, its metamorphosis, its metropolitan ambitions, exert a strong power even over the disaffected. As the song goes, Berlin is a city in which many people who now live in foreign corners of the world have left a metaphorical suitcase behind. Thus, the next time I a pay a visit, it shall not be in the vein of a pilgrimage, in search for nostalgia or for comparative studies. I shall be a foreign tourist with a perfect command of German and an open mind. Perhaps, if I manage to distance myself from the past and look at the city like a first-time visitor, I shall be able to give Berlin a new place in my affections.

I did go back. In ninety-eight. As a 'foreign' tourist. Equipped with the latest urban map, I explored the new Berlin, or was being shown around by friends. And I had to admit: the city has not only been given a new facelift, but some phenomenal building work in its former eastern sector has created a new business, banking and commercial centre, in which shops, offices and apartments have found keen occupants. Super-modern glass and steel high-rise complexes have risen on and around Potsdamer Platz and Alexanderplatz - an area which before the war had been the commercial heart of Berlin, before it was flattened by Allied bombs. In DDR times it had largely been left waste or been turned into the notorious no-man's land along the Wall. I remember an earlier visit to the area: huge cranes sticking out into the air, resembling slow-wagging forefingers; a team of pile-drivers thumping away, construction traffic whirling up clouds of dust. Whatever traditionalists may now think of the final architectural urban show-piece, the very logistics of building a new city centre on limited space is simply mind-boggling. However, those among us who remember what the area looked like before the war, will find it difficult to hang onto past images. But then, nostalgia has no place on the soil which is seen as the heart of National Socialism. Perhaps it was time to change the landscape and to bury unpleasant witnesses under concrete.

Berliners acknowledge that their city is full of contradiction. It lies on Germany's eastern periphery, being both an eastern and western shop-window of politics. Despite - or perhaps because - of its chequered past, visitors find its

11

charm endearing. Besides, they say, 'Everything is so neat and tidy, so regulated and organised. Everything seems to function. And what about their public transport? It runs to a timetable you can set your watch to.' And they might add, 'Fancy, people are not allowed to step on public lawns, and under a certain by-law, carpets must not be beaten, nor grass cut, on Sundays and during *Mittagszeit* (siesta-time).'

As for me, I am proud of the achievements of my *Heimatstadt*. I admit, though, that I have failed to give my place of birth a new place of affection. That is why, in 2008, the last time I visited this throbbing, kaleidoscopic city, I picked up my suitcase of sepia memories and took it home. Here, its contents will survive.

'Goodbye, Berlin.'

1990 - 2008

PS: What I miss in my rural Kentish life is Berlin's scintillating cultural scene, which may command the world's top artists. But then there are compensations, albeit of the modest kind. And anyway, I have long outgrown my love for Nusstörtchen.

2011

I'VE TRIED EVERYTHING

Believe me, I've tried everything. I've clapped my hands as if applauding my favourite tennis player for winning a decisive point; I snarled like a Rottweiler, furiously drummed on an empty water butt or waved a black cloth like an avian predator's wings. All to no avail. I'm fighting a losing battle against a colony of wood-pigeons, a raunchy male bird being the main reason for my aggressive antics.

An obvious newcomer to the local clan of the genus *Columbae*, and the size of an overfed drake, he will sit in my garden high up on the willow tree or on top of the TV aerial, calling for a mate and authoritatively claiming his territory. In doing so, he produces sounds that resemble those of an asthmatic parrot in love with its own voice. No wonder then that his off-key, repetitive calls will creep under my scalp, and etch themselves irritatingly into my consciousness.

Take the best of a British summer day, a day to sit in the garden, allowing the soul to soak up tranquillity and the mind to spin Andrew Marvell's 'green thoughts in a green shade'. Yet the self-proclaimed Lord of the Willow will soon make sure that his din - which always ends in a *crescendo* - digs up the worst in me: a killer instinct normally surfacing only at the sight of rats, big black beetles, cockroaches, wasps and garden pests.

Meanwhile, from the tops of surrounding trees, and playing a game of 'change the perch', a chorus of lady pigeons and their youngsters will split the air with commensurate sounds on their own scale. This is the moment when most uncharitable thoughts are rushing through my mind. They advocate the use of a stone-armed catapult or other missile launcher.

My next-door neighbour, consulted about a suitable deterrent, replied, 'Oh, but they are such lovely creatures. I feed them every day.' 'What about their infernal noise from dawn to nightfall?' I asked, only to be told that her man was hard-of-hearing. As my other neighbour would not hear a thrush singing *fortissimo* without switching on her hearing-aid full volume, I am thus resigned to suffer every day the torture of nerve-racking decibels. And since the resident colony of little brutes around the village start greeting Aurora and each other at 4 am in summer, I shall have to keep my bedroom window shut at night or invest in a pair of ear-plugs, neither of which are desirable options.

Wood-pigeons are classified as 'doves' alongside other species of pigeons. They are commonly seen as symbols of peace and gentleness. The Bible speaks of the dove returning to the Ark with an olive branch in its beak, which to Noah is the good news that *terra firma* is emerging from the flooded land. In this sense, the dove stands for the renewal of life on earth; for God having made peace with surviving mankind. However, whether truth or legend, my wood-pigeons have no saving graces. They do not keep their beaks shut when told, nor do they bring me good news. On the contrary, the ominous, whimper-like cooing of baby pigeons drums home to me the message that yet another clutch of eggs has hatched.

Mind you, if my molesters' vocal performances were done *cantabile*, softly, say, at the full hour each day, and if the virile, loud-throated macho specimen should drop dead one day, it would be a different matter altogether. Until such a time, the pigeon clan is not only vocally and territorially in command, not caring a hoot about their noise-plagued human host, but the speed with which they increase also makes for a mind-boggling prospect. Who knows, one day - along with their more gentle-voiced cousins, the doves of Noah's Ark fame - they may no longer be ranked as the proverbial emblem of peace. One day, in a freak evolutionary process having grown even feistier and more aggressive, they may act like Hitchcock's Birds.

PS: It would seem that I have not tried everything after all. As a last resort, I have borrowed my grandson's water-gun and I am now practising water combat in defence of my realm and sanity.

2006

I STILL WARM MY TEAPOT

I was born in the mid-1920s, which means that to the present generation I am 'ancient'. Well, judging by my wrinkles, my walking stick, and the tiredness of eyes and skin, I am. And the way I am sticking to some inherited practices shows that I still have one foot in the last century. Yet my mind is still as agile and questioning as a child's, and when I hear a dance tune from the Forties and Fifties, every fibre of my being wants to move to the rhythm. I may have laid to rest my dreams of sleeping under a desert sky, snow-gliding through Canadian brown bear territory, sailing down the Yangtze or following the footprints of Wilfred Thesinger or Colin Thubron, but like millions of other old people I am not wholly stuck in the past, but enjoy the convenience of fridges, freezers and washing machines, as well as other devices of modern technology.

However, I admit defeat, if not a *soupçon* of hostility, towards computers; to websites, online and e-mail communication, all of which - the ubiquitous textphone and brutalising computer games included - rob the user, if not the addict, of time to think, write letters to a friend and socially interact. While I admit that computers are time-saving and informative, and from a national security point of view are now indispensable, I see their impact on society as comparable to the Iron Age, industrialisation, antibiotics, synthetics, television, space technology, McDonald's and IKEA. My reluctance to embrace the benefits and perils of computer screen, mouse and the maze of keys - one of which, I hear, if pressed in error can wipe out whole pages of text - is not senile stubbornness, but may lie in one of my genes which made higher maths and physics non-subjects at school for me, and in adult life did not allow me to proceed from electric typewriter to word processing and internet research.

While I should not like to be without my basic mobile phone and 'automatic' car, and selective radio and television entertainment, I have faithfully, and often subconsciously, retained many customs of my mother's and grandmother's time. In an age of quick pharmaceutical remedies and rampant consumerism, these may well induce smiles of indulgence in the modern woman whose parents have not left a legacy of certain conservative, time-proven practices that have withstood the rapid technical, medical and social development of our age.

Laugh, if you may, but I still warm my teapot with boiling water and keep the brew under a cosy while it 'draws'; I still strip my bed in the morning, to air, and I wash 'delicates' and jumpers by hand. I mend anything mendable, instead of replacing repairable items straight away - a custom which may well have been ingrained by the harsh war and post-war years, when 'new-for-old' was not on the survival agenda. (Today, when I sew on a button, I remember my grandmother's box of mother-of-pearl, coloured or oddly-shaped buttons, a treasure trove which for the child, provided hours of play.) Oh, and I still hang up my clothes and put trees into my leather shoes. Now, how *passé*, how positively outmoded can you get?

Also, call me annoyingly *bourgeois*, but I never drink from a bottle, like construction workers, puerile 'bingers' and EastEnders' Queen Vic drinkers. For many purists and conservative drinkers, this 21st century informality would seem socially unacceptable. Also, the way many people drink wine nowadays won't earn them any points, as they tend to grip their glass like an earthenware mug, when - just as I was taught - any discerning wine lover will hold his by its stem, which lends a certain grace to the act and flatters a good vintage.

I am positively old-fashioned at the dining table. When I have a hot meal in company, I will not be using my knife and fork like a conductor, in order to emphasise or argue a point, while munching and talking, elbow on the table, the kind of mannerism now often seen in students' dining halls, in restaurants and on television. I know I am only one of my contemporaries who deplore the decline of good table manners. Moreover, who still uses a serviette? Well, I for one do not fancy a meal without a table napkin. Mine even commands its heirloom silver ring. After all, a fair-sized napkin soaks up the telling dribbles of tomato or carrot soup, the greasy impact of a flighty chip, the colourful stains of red berries and the odd gravy spritzer; a napkin is also handy to wipe your mouth with, instead of using the back of your hand.

I also leave a gratuity with my milkman and postman at Christmas, as most householders in German-speaking countries do, although many of my neighbours see such seasonal tips as an unnecessary expenditure.

Where my hold on to practices I grew up with is most effective is in the home treatment of colds, coughs and stomach upsets and - in the first line of defence - of other minor conditions that are likely to clear up without a visit to the GP and without antibiotics. While the latter may shorten an illness or even save a life, they also come with various side effects. 'Patient help yourself first' has, therefore, always been my motto. When I have a sore throat or a troublesome cough I treat it with hot, honeyed drinks, an over-the-counter expectorant and soothing lozenges; at the first sign of a chest infection, I apply a hot poultice to my chest and prescribe myself a day in bed or in front of the television, the usual patient-comforters by my side. When my stomach or guts cry for help, I keep to a one-day diet of porridge, dry toast, mint tea and grated apple. It always does the job. Alright, I may sound utterly, incorrigibly, mid-nineteenth century, but these simple home remedies have stood the test of time. Some go back to our elderly Jewish family doctor, the kind of GP who, sadly, is now extinct. He not only made house calls, but also cooled feverish foreheads and prescribed hot oil poultices for ear and chest infections. He smiled and reassured, and it was understood that he would follow up his visit. When, one day, he stopped coming, we learned that he had become a victim of Hitler's racial policies.

One chapter of my mother's and grandmother's household bible dealt with ironing. Both ladies prided themselves on the state of their linen cupboard: bed and table linen neatly folded and lying edge to edge. Having first been boiled in a copper vessel on the hob, each item was hand-washed on a metal board, before being hung out for drying. Large bed sheets and tablecloths were then taken to a mangle, the remainder ironed with dedication - even tea towels. Perhaps not unexpectedly, I adopted the old laundry practice. Following years of out-of-suitcase living and ever-changing abodes, once I was married and had a family, I would first continue with the familiar laundering routine, before being introduced to a washing machine and tumble drier. However, I still iron every item - even tea towels, and my linen cupboard resembles neatly-stacked supermarket shelves.

As far as fashion trends are concerned, I had to make allowances over the years. Down, or up, went my hemlines as to the dictates of fashion, yet never so high as to expose my thighs to fresh air and whistles from building sites. I also never wore a whale-bone corset like my grandmother, never sported a pair of black lace panties or - God forbid - a stringy, bare-nearly-all thong. Until recently I had never heard of 'Pilates', and I wish there was a dictionary for all those new-fangled, trendy words which are part of teenagers' and newspaper columnists' vocabulary. Yet when trousers became *à la mode*, I took to them immediately, while my necklines gradually lost their puritanical look. However, I still like wearing pearls, the kind of class-defining jewellery which my mother and grandmother considered to be the alpha and omega of a lady's smart attire.

They say 'old habits die hard'. This may be a truism. Old people merely like to stick to whatever makes them feel comfortable and connects them with their past - customs that despite all beneficial advances, have proved their value.

And now it's time for tea. The kettle is boiling. My friends tell me that I make a good 'cuppa', yet none has ever asked me whether I use quality loose tea or PG tea bags.

2006

18

A TRIBUTE

Poets have immortalised the Great Achilles, Ulysses and Alexander; they have lauded kings and queens, written eulogies about Love, Life and Nature. They have praised the Christian God and other religious deities. Many a stanza has also been written about the glory of the garden, and who does not remember Kubla Khan's pleasure dome, Keats' Ode to a Nightingale, or, from Wordsworth's enchanted pen, the 'host of golden daffodils'?

In our society, we pay tribute largely to secular delights, many of which are of our own making, born out of greed, vanity and all too often a nihilistic, self-indulgent attitude to life. We take for granted the workings of our body, the obedience of our limbs to the command of our brain. But whoever pays tribute to their hands, whether they tell of a lifetime of manual labour, pen-wielding, white-collar or artistic occupations, or point to a silver-spooned, soft-gloved *milieu*?

Let us be honest: we take the power and dexterity of our hands for granted. We think of them as indispensable serfs, and watch with a sense of sad acceptance, their knuckles growing knobbly over the years, their skin indelibly marked with coffee-stained blotches and stretching over prominent veins - over old hands. People who by whatever misadventure have lost a hand will readily agree that even a state-of-the-art prosthesis cannot replace a hand's servitude, its agility and sensitivity.

Looking closely at my own hands, their fabric of bone, tendons and network of veins, I know I cannot disguise their age. In an unflattering light, they seem to belong to a mummy. Now covered by gossamer skin, inelastic in texture, their veins are standing out like bas-reliefs, deep blue, unsightly. Yet, they are wearing their looks with dignity, knowing that even a million dollar ring could not belie their age. In my eyes they are beautiful... They are my best friends. They have scrubbed floors, cleaned up vomit, dressed putrefying wounds; they used hammer, saw and paintbrush in DIY jobs and, before the advent of washing machines, laundered with the help of a copper boiler, wooden spoon and a metal wash-board. They handled delicate instruments, threaded needles, crocheted and in feats of labour wrote and typed millions of words.

They also held my babies to my breast, cradled, cuddled, spoon-fed, wiped away tears; they lit candles on birthday cakes, applied first aid to wounded knees, stroked away pain and cooled feverish foreheads. Also, all too often in my life, when I faced an emotional or physical crisis, my hands would fold in silent supplication. And to this day I recall how they caressed a lover, closed the eyes of my mother and father, played *études* on the piano and held the reins of a horse.

Although I was once offered a handshake by the then President of West Germany, a warm greeting by the Lutheran pastor and concentration camp survivor, Martin Niemöller, the powerful grip by one of the richest men of *generalissimo* Franco's Spain, and the limp hand by a former icon of Germany's post-war economy, my right hand did not give itself airs. On the contrary. Both my hands are still stubborn weeders of flower-beds, and they are very much at home at the hob. They still skilfully wield a lady's make-up paraphernalia, offer a resting place to butterflies and delicately snip off a rose. In genial teamwork, they steer my car, hold bridge cards and wrap up presents.

They are also responsible hands, for they have never pulled a trigger, assaulted another human being or, in the biblical sense, washed themselves in the face of injustice. Similarly, although sometimes feeling the urge, they have never stuck up two fingers in a mute four-letter gesture. Yet whether moaning with arthritic pain, and on arctic winter days mindful of how on a war-time refugee trek they only just escaped frostbite, my hands remain happy and servile.

With a flourish they have typed this tribute and are now signing off.

2007

IT'S ONLY NATURAL

In William Welby's 1937 book on nudism, 'It's Only Natural', the author (himself a follower of the cult) portrays nudists as respectable, ordinary people who, unlike cranks and faddists, see health benefits in the exposure of skin to air and light. Contrary to general belief, he says, they don't like being seen naked in public and they get no sexual thrills out of seeing each other unclothed. Complete nudity, he maintains, is pure and chaste, as it is in art.

Well, how times have changed, if the latest news item is anything to go by. In a rapid growth of nudism, the cult is alleged to have taken on Hugh Walpole's creed as their logo: 'When I take my clothes off, I cast off my cares.'

Germany, long in the forefront of nudist culture, and with special beaches in Baltic Sea resorts, or parts of city parks, long assigned to practitioners of naturism, appears to have updated the movement to the twenty-first century by widening its permissible moral perimeter. Thus, in February this year (2008), two *Times* editorials were quick to comment on a German news item which had all the ingredients of a farce: 'Nudists rush to book, as the first clothes-free flights put bottoms on seats', ran one explosive opening line. As February had only just dawned, it could not have been an April Fool's joke. Well, it wasn't. Apparently, nudists from across the world have chartered a 50-passenger flight scheduled to leave Erfurt in eastern Germany for the naturist beach on the Baltic island of Usedom on July 5. Passengers will have to check in the clothes they are wearing together with their hold baggage.

Immediately, questions surface: where will they leave their money and wallets? Will there be problems fastening seat belts? And what if, due to some mid-air engine hitch over the Baltic Sea, they were told to don their life-jackets and prepare for an emergency landing on water? According to *The Times*,

21

chutes would then 'spill out ready-peeled human beings to startled sharks'. What, sharks in the Baltic Sea? A hilarious hypothesis.

Another question beckons: what if mischievous baggage handlers 'lost' passengers' suitcases? Surely this would set the stage for slapstick comedy.

On reading about the entrepreneurial pilot scheme of the Ossi (East German) flight operator, I conjured up images of bare bottoms hugging seats - neither an aesthetic nor a hygienic way of travel. But have no fear, the airline wants to put a special cloth on every seat, allegedly to prevent backsides from sticking to them. However, although comfort will thus be guaranteed at one's lower end, I shiver at the thought of the cabin air growing increasingly cooler once the aircraft is gaining height and, in the resulting chill, there being nothing but the bare arms and shoulders of strangers in the neighbouring seats to provide a modicum of warmth.

It would seem that there is a market for nudist flights in Germany, as bookings have come in from as far as Japan and New Zealand. Now, I ask you, what possesses cult-followers to go for the ultimate experience of flying naked? Surely, even early *Homo sapiens* soon donned a loin cloth to cover private parts. Do nude passengers hope to find a special in-flight intimacy and solidarity, a heightened sense of purpose? Don't huge bottoms and bellies, sagging breasts and shrunken male appendages provide an antidote to nudism? A turn-off? After all, not everyone has the body of a Greek god or goddess. Besides, with their clothing packed away in the plane's hold, how can they avoid causing a stir on arrival or departure? What if, by chance or through some organisational oversight by ground staff, the naked onslaught were to come face to face with, say, a red-carpeted VIP or a visiting bishop? What if they were to cross the path of a class of primary school children with buckets and spades, waiting to board a holiday flight and being wholly unprepared for their first voyeuristic experience? And what if word were to leak out to the press - might not half the population of Erfurt and Usedom be thronging the airports, no doubt joined by a coterie of prim moralists and anti-nudism protesters?

Flashers exposing themselves to a football crowd or elsewhere in public may have a psychological or libido-related problem. Nudists, flying naked, might merely wish to reinforce or demonstrate the 'naturalness' of the cult.

While the flight does not sound like an endurance test, it is unlikely to kindle erotic titillation. Passengers will not be served hot drinks, as spillage might cause nasty burns. And no more than a sip of chilled wine will be served with the nibbles, so as not to upset the required non-committal behaviour of passengers. Anyway, so the organisers emphasised, cabin staff would watch out for any (unlikely) impropriety. Their charges will even have to restrain themselves from casting glances around, sizing up fellow passengers. Eyes straight ahead shall be the order of the flight, and no hanky-panky, please. Hands may hold a glass, a book or a copy of the *Frankfurter Allgemeine*. No 'girlie' magazines shall be allowed on board.

The whole venture will, of course, make headlines in both broadsheets and tabloids; the media will run amok and the two airports see an increased police presence. Not that there is a German law against flying naked, although it may be illegal to board, or step from, an aircraft without clothes. I bet some lawyers are already at work, searching for a loophole in relevant by-laws, unless Heath and Safety get there first.

I, for one, shall be following up the news from Erfurt this summer. Meanwhile, what is bugging me, is the attitude of the flight attendants. Clothed as they are, will they be comfortable serving passengers 'in the buff'? Or will they... After all, it would only be natural.

October 2008. July 5 came and went. No further news emerged about the flight. Did the morality police cancel it or did passengers, in some clandestine operation, board under cover of darkness? I'm afraid we shall never know.

The Times, September 25, 2009
'Not content with a nudist airline and a strip-off hotel in the Black Forest region, Germany has announced an official 11-mile (18 km) hiking path for naked backpackers...!'

Mosquitoes will have a feast.

OF MICE AND WOMAN AND OTHER CREATURES

I do not have a dog, but I am very fond of canines, whatever their breed and size. And somehow they seem to like me, my scent or whatever clicks in a dog's mind, saying, 'Ah, there's a friend.' Dogs will come up to me, or allow me to approach and stroke them, even those vexing creatures which growl or bark rabidly at strangers, or which exhibit other behavioural problems.

Cats, too, may have a soft spot for me. Having sized me up, and sensing no hostility, they will curl around my legs with instant affection.

With birds I have a special relationship. Birds are finding my garden a safe nesting and feeding site, and during the gardening season, they have long accepted their host's frequent presence as something unavoidable and posing no threat.

Birds fascinate me. Perhaps it is their freedom in flight, which touches a chord in me, their ability to wing themselves into the air at will. Deep inside me there has always been a desire to be able to cruise through the skies like a snowgoose, a seagull or a swallow. To feel free of whatever shackles man to earth.

In winter I regularly feed my resident feathered guests, and this has rewarded me with the loyalty of robins, thrushes, blackbirds, starlings, blue tits, willow warblers and hedge sparrows. Come seven o'clock, or whenever winter mornings are growing light, they will be waiting at a respectable distance from the feeding tray or hopping excitedly from branch to branch. And woe betide me if I'm late. The ensuing twittering and chirping could wake up a heavy sleeper. And every morning it is a fat blackbird which first rushes to the scene, as if to say that when there is no worm to catch, the early bird will secure the choicest items of man's offering.

However, I have no sympathy for garden pests, and I positively cringe at the sight of big black beetles, giant spiders and earwigs which have a habit of slipping through the narrowest of spaces from the garden and garage, from behind skirting boards, through drains and other structural apertures.

Spiders I never kill, as much as I abhor their multi-legged appearance. Instead, I have developed a humane method of reprisal which allows me to deposit them gently in the garden. Earwigs and other nasty creepy-crawlies, which find their way into the house, are not so lucky.

Fortunately, my property does not accommodate armies of cockroaches, the endemic pest in the Far East, some European and other countries, where lack of domestic hygiene and a sub-tropical or hot climate create ideal living and breeding conditions for these monsters.

To see them foraging in the kitchen, as they did in ours in Hong Kong, used to seize me with horror. With their armoured backs, they are difficult to swat or trample underfoot, which makes each slaying attempt a harrowing experience.

Other visitors which I will not tolerate in the house or in the garage are mice. While low winter temperatures will make them seek man's warm habitation, particularly if there are tasty titbits lying around or are easily accessible in nightly excursions, man cannot afford to give board and lodgings to rodents. Mice are easy prey to cats, but they are seldom spotted feeding or in flight. They are also canny and most prolific in the breeding department. As for catching them, nothing will do but a trap, unless one takes recourse to some drastic and unnecessarily cruel killing methods.

The first winter in my new house remains memorable for the ubiquitous droppings mice were leaving in rooms overnight. Their scouting range pointed to a systematic search of furniture, window sills, bookshelves, kitchen larder and worktops. One night, lying half awake, I was startled by a soft touch on my cheek. When I put on the light, a mouse took a giant leap from my pillow onto the carpet and disappeared in a flash. Now, this was surely the last straw, I thought, feeling aghast at having the privacy of my bedroom invaded by a rodent. Male or female, it may well have developed a liking for a woman's warm, night-creamed cheek, but such a gesture of affection or curiosity was decidedly going too far.

I acquired a humane mousetrap which soon cleared up the infestation of the house, and when mice subsequently made their presence known in the adjoining garage, where they managed to bite through waxed paper bags of bird food, I installed another trap. Every night for two weeks I thus caught two of these scavengers. It must indeed have been a large family. With their stomachs full of cheese or biscuit crumbs, the victims would then have no choice but to await whatever manner of disposal their human trapper had in mind.

In time, I admit, I grew quite fond of my prisoners, because once I had seen their pink eyes, their quivering whiskers and thread-like long tails, I could not help feeling moved by their incarceration. Giant woman suddenly felt very mean.

Whenever I was unable to relocate them shortly after discovery, I made their waiting time on what must have felt like death row easy for them, by dropping some biscuit crumbs into their cages. A last meal before their execution? Indeed not. Every morning I took my catch by car to the nearest field and opened the trap door. At first, the mice would test the air, viewing the long grass at eye level, perhaps not believing that freedom was imminent, rather than death by drowning or other inhumane methods, before they jumped out and disappeared in the green jungle as if chased by a cat. Whenever the weather was frosty, I threw some bread or cheese after them - provisions to last them until they had found another abode or source of food. That is how soft-hearted I am, or rather, how daft I had become with regard to mice.

I thus believe that unless the heavenly powers allow me to pass through the Pearly Gates at the end of my days, I shall be made welcome not only in the Elysian Fields of birds and spiders, but also in the celestial sanctuary of mice.

2006

HAPPINESS UNDER THE MICROSCOPE

Happiness variously stands for joy, delight, pleasure and other emotions associated with a lofty state of mind. In time-worn fashion, one may be 'on top of the world', 'in seventh heaven' or 'on cloud nine'. Other metaphors may be used to describe astral flights of feelings, of being mentally and physically airborne. Indeed, it is man's fundamental right to pursue happiness, and to attach a value to it as to the golden fleece.

However, as we get older and wiser, we realise how fragile this state is. That it is often no more than a mirage, and in its material form does not touch the soul.

Seneca, the stoic Roman philosopher, goes further. He is not happy, who depends for happiness on external things, he says, for worldly goods are brittle. Only joy that comes from within is true happiness.

It takes some of us half a lifetime, if not longer, to come to that conclusion. As one of life's perennial survivors, I might add that once we have learnt how little we need to be basically 'happy', a life without materialistic criteria will bring true contentment. But to gain such insight, we may perhaps first have to earn a few pearls of wisdom.

Now that I find myself in the wintry season of my life, I sometimes wake up in the morning, wishing I could embrace the new day with the sheer delight of being alive. Yet I still remember the years when I stretched out my arms to the rising sun, smiling, and impatient to gather the gifts of another day. Then, new experiences were waiting for me around every corner, as were challenges and, in the process of dealing with them, eye-openers of self-discovery. On such days I would walk taller, life was wonderful and I knew that I was happy. And even when capricious fate would kick me, or knock me down, I always knew that the joys of life were only biding their time. Happiness in my younger self did not come with a sell-by date; it needed no sustenance, no commitments. It was there for the taking.

So what happened?

I may be presumptuous trying to analyse a state of being which has been diversely described as an orgasm of the senses, an ecstasy of the spirit and a sublime experience of the soul. Many philosophers have attempted to dissect it as in a post-mortem exercise, but a human condition that comes in so many different shapes, shades and decibels surely defies an anatomical examination. Besides, what to a multi-millionaire is the affordability of the world's luxuries, to a player on the stock exchange a financial coup, to a businessman a successful take-over bid, is to a homeless person a bed for the night, a proper meal and that extra pound or two in his pocket. Equally, a man may see happiness in a pint of lager at the pub, a drug addict in his fix, a student in the passing of a vital exam. In certain women's magazines and Mills & Boon books, the happy end is synonymous with love and a proposal of marriage. Christians may find their spiritual high in Sunday Communion, some people in a lottery win, others in that decisive goal of their favourite football team.

In small children, happiness is surely at its most pristine. Who has not seen a toddler's face break into the sunniest of smiles while he is chasing a coloured balloon or trying to catch with his hand an iridescent soap bubble? Or if, following several unsuccessful attempts, he manages to put the last building block on a miniature Eiffel Tower without seeing it collapse? In the young, a cuddly teddy bear, a favourite dessert, a piggy-back ride on Daddy, as well as that lovely new toy, will achieve the same result.

I remember childhood years when happiness came on my birthday not so much with presents, but with my favourite meal: jacket potatoes with fried rashers of bacon, followed by iced vanilla soup crowned with mounds of stiffly-beaten egg white.

As a teenager during the war, I recall heydays of happiness, spent boating on a dreamy lake, and swimming naked at sunset in water that was as clear and smooth as liquid glass. I can still feel the joy of riding my bike along the river Havel, or skiing over virgin snow in the mountains. While living in the children's home I felt exuberant when temperatures and a stern matron allowed us to change our long, woollen hose for knee stockings or, what bliss, for ankle socks. As for the frugal institutional table, blueberries with milk and sugar, *Quark* with cranberries, and ham rolls would evoke sighs of delight.

During the later months of the war, happiness was the knowledge of having survived yet another air raid. It was, if one was lucky, a plate of hot cabbage soup and a slice of rough bread which would temporarily allay the constant pangs of hunger. On the refugee trek, it was the realisation that my youth and fighting spirit provided me with the necessary mental and physical stamina to endure days without food or rest in arctic temperatures, while around me older people and children kept collapsing, to freeze to death at the roadside.

As if it were yesterday, I remember the crisp morning early in May 1945, when I stepped into the garden, where feisty candles of lilac provided a feast for the eyes, and the orchestrated song of birds brought aural joy. Following the cessation of street fighting, shelling and sniping, the small town in western Germany, in which I had come to live towards the end of the war, was utterly quiet at this hour. For me, it was a moment when I experienced a shudder of happiness - the future was opening up, one that held hope and a new beginning. This sensation repeated itself a few days later, when on hearing that Hitler had died and the war was over, the country froze into a stunned silence. Then - with all the weeping and praying and smiling and embracing over - Hope picked up the first brick from the rubble.

I later shaped my thoughts, and presumably those of millions of surviving Germans, into the poem And Then There Was Silence. I daresay it could stand today for the emotions of millions of people in war-torn countries once hostilities have ended.

...And then there was silence

And the sudden calm
grew into a dome of stillness
the echoes of Hell
retreated into the archives
of future scenarios
and uneasy dreams.

Eyes,
for years assaulted
with apocalyptic sights
feasted on new-born images,
on young smiles,
spring flowers
and pink apple blossoms

Dust-filled lungs
greedily inhaled
the sweet scents of May,
thoughts limped to a halt,
threw away crutches,
raced forward, skipped
and somersaulted

Ears,
dulled by the cacophony of war
picked up the song of thrushes,
rejoiced in a child's prattle,
in the sound of phantom bells
ringing in peace
from empty belfries

Hope
sprouted like dandelions
from the heap of rubble,
millions,
among wreaths and daffodils,
embraced, prayed, smiled or wept
then picked up the first brick in the silence.

31

Whilst living with friends on Mallorca in the early Fifties, I attempted to read *La Filosofia del Felicidad* by an eminent Spanish writer. I don't know what had prompted me to buy a paperback copy of the book, in which the author tried to analyse happiness. Perhaps, for the first time in my life, I was looking beyond accepted boundaries, questioning and examining sentiments that were part of the human psyche. It was a time when I was happy, detached, if not wholly released, from the tribulations of earlier years. Here, under a Spanish sky, happiness was being young and in love; it was waking every morning without a big lump of angst in my throat. Happiness was hot sunshine, unspoilt beaches and a sea which glistened at sunrise and blushed under the setting sun. It was giant, juicy peaches, Sangria, fish soup and Mallorcan music, and at night the swarms of fireflies dancing through the sultry air that was heavily scented with the breath of *Bougainvillaea* and other subtropical blooms.

My memory has preserved highlights of happiness as if they were gemstones.

I remember the day the man whom I had been dating for the best part of two years asked me to marry him. For days I could not take the glee off my face. I was looking forward to a home, children and, yes, financial security.

I vividly recall the birth of my three sons. The extreme maternal delight and pride that suffused me. I would repeatedly look into the mirror, expecting my face to have changed. But all it reflected was a radiant smile.

The euphoria I experienced following each delivery repeated itself, when a major London publisher accepted the manuscript of my first book, and the day I saw it in print.

Since those days, happiness has come soft-soled and in pastel shades. It is tinged with the pride of what my sons have achieved in their careers, and with the joy of seeing my grandchildren growing up.

Indeed, as the years now seem to pass with lightning speed, and my limited mobility and certain other health problems further narrow the scope of activities and expectations, the more humble things in everyday life increasingly manage to provide morsels of happiness. I may no longer find gold nuggets at my feet, but there will come moments when happiness in the guise of contentment touches me with gloved hands - times when it scatters mites of joy between the rocks of living. Such as a beam of sunshine wedging itself through dark bulbous clouds, a difficult completed Times crossword, a day without pain or angst, a visit from family or friends. It stands, ultimately, for books, Bach, a game of bridge and something, however modest, to look forward to.

I also find a childish pleasure in watching my resident bird population pecking away at what I provide for them; I experience a gardener's joy on seeing spring and summer unfolding, and autumn celebrating its season with russet colours. And there may come moments when such flushes of happiness sober up a defeatist spirit.

True happiness may be difficult to define. For most people, it lies in secular joy. Some will compare it to an ephemeral state, to a mayfly; the pious will see it as not being of this world. Helen Keller once went further: 'When one door of happiness closes,' she said, 'another one opens. But we may look so long at the closed door that we don't see the one which has been opened for us.'

Perhaps it is the one through which we may perceive and count our graces...

THE GOOD OLD DAYS

'Praising what is lost, makes remembrance dear'

Shakespeare
(All's Well That Ends Well)

The good old days. Were they really that good? Or is nostalgia for a vanished time unrealistic and unfair?

Like many older folk, and in tandem with many a present-day feature writer examining past and present cultural and social trends, I sometimes muse about 'the good old days'. Looking closely at what today is considered to be outmoded or downright primitive, and what is now accepted practice or seen as enhancing daily life, one has to admit that progress often extracts a heavy price for the benefits it bestows on mankind. As every potent drug has its side effects, so many a new invention or scientific breakthrough has also taken something away from society, often in some subtle way. In the landscape of the last century, I see progress rising like redwood trees, yet like many other folk I am not blind to the blots it has left behind, here and there.

Nonetheless, many are the blessings none of us would want to be without today.

As I picked up my pint of milk from the doorstep this morning, I remembered the time when one fetched unpasteurised milk from a horse-drawn cart. The milkman would just open a tap and, like draught beer, the milk would flow into one's jug.

I was about nine years old when my fascination with the milk-cart made me hitch onto its rear one day, to enjoy a free ride down the road. Someone must have seen my bold behaviour and reported it to my parents. In what would today be a punishable offence, my father produced a reed cane and gave me a good whacking. Needless to say, I never repeated such a daredevil act.

As a housewife, I recall the huge sink and corrugated washing-board, the copper boiler, crude soap, and the mangle whose handle used to squeak like a raunchy frog. On wash-days hands got red and chapped, and since German *Waschküchen*[1] used to be sited in basements, strong arms and backs were needed to heave the wet laundry upstairs, to be hung in backyards, gardens or communal lofts. As washing machines gradually took the sweat out of laundering, so today's mothers find nappy-changing a one-minute task. Terry-towel squares no longer have to be soaked, rinsed, boiled and hand-washed, and they are no longer flapping like pennants on washing lines in the wind. Surely someone ought to have been knighted for inventing the disposable product.

Just as washing machines and tumble dryers are now making light of laundering, so other domestic chores have been eased by electrical appliances which even fifty years ago would have been in the experimental stage or of a primitive, unwieldy design. Then we were unaware of, or still tampering with, what is now an essential part of modern living, and of what is being forecast further to change our lifestyle.

Indeed, science and technology seem to know no bounds. Thus, in a society in which few taboos are left, and in which many voices proclaim that God is dead, there is no telling how far human intelligence will try, or be able, to thrust itself into the Great Unknown.

Today, most households have a fridge or a fridge-freezer. Yet it was not that long ago that the ice-man came with his cart, selling big blocks of ice for box-like domestic containers no larger than a bedside locker. I can still hear the hooves of the old mare clattering down the cobbled street, in which a passing car would turn heads.

While few of us would want to be without the medical advances or the information technology of our time, all morally

---

[1] Laundry rooms

sound, peace-loving citizens must surely wish that The Bomb, and the whole arsenal of sophisticated weaponry, had never left the drawing board.

The good old days were not so good when compared with the achievements of modern medicine, which not only make us live longer, but also allow surgeons successfully to perform operations which tread formerly inaccessible ground. Doctors have an ever-widening range of drugs to effect cures, soothe or eliminate pain - all of which would have been the stuff of science fiction a century ago. I well remember the years before antibiotic and quick-fix medicines, when home remedies had to be relied upon. Handed down from one generation to another, they boosted the healing process of minor illnesses and often dispensed with the doctor altogether. Hot oil compresses for chest or ear infections, castor oil for constipation, inhalations for coughs and congested sinuses, strained oatmeal, grated apple and camomile tea for diarrhoea were just some of the home cures. They might have taken longer to act, but they left no side effects.

Progress in dental medicine has taken the horrors out of the drill and forceps. Judging by some recent repair work in the dentist's chair, the excruciating pain I often had to endure as a teenager and young woman would nowadays equate with medieval torture.

Today, television, videos and CDs provide home entertainment. Youngsters go berserk over PlayStations and computer games, while the Net - apart from its obvious advantage in the field of communications - also claims much of the leisure time of the screen-obsessed.

Somehow one cannot get away from the hallelujah cries of people who are mastering the new technology. Laid-back and elderly citizens who missed the chance to upgrade their typing skills are daily bombarded with alien technical terms like website, online, Windows, megabytes, internet, dot-coms, e-mail, cyberspace, RAM, bugs and modems, not forgetting that little domestic vermin, the mouse, which is allowed to rest on a padded bed.

I, for one, am still writing on an electric typewriter, some of whose special functions still confuse me. I take it, therefore, that I have 'missed the boat'. However, I am quite content to leave all on-screen operations to those who did catch on to it, particularly that new breed of computer wizards who are roaming in the latest technology as in outer space.

In my younger days in Germany, a two-band radio was like a hearth, around which the family gathered in the evenings, to listen to music or Hitler's speeches, and to what my parents did not yet realise was heavily censored and manipulated news. I might play cards with my father for 1 Reichspfennig a point, listen to my mother playing the piano, or pretend to read clever illustrated books. After school I played marbles, did the 'skip and hop', flew kites, and learned how to swim and ice-skate. I also collected horse chestnuts and carved them into baskets. In December I got busy making Christmas presents from fabric, paper, cardboard and plywood.

With a smile I recall whole villages I designed with a miniature wooden church, school, shop, cottages, farm buildings and domestic animals. No limits were set to the imagination. For special treats there would be a Shirley Temple film, Lanterna Magica slides of Struwwelpeter, a visit to the zoo, the circus or to one of the famous Berlin Scala's Revues. Silhouette games and Punch and Judy shows would also create special islands of happiness.

How simple childhood pleasures were, how innocent, yet how they cultivated the imagination.

Once I had become a fluent reader, I let my imagination steer me precariously through the adventures of Tarzan, Tom Sawyer and Winnetou, the chief of the Apaches. During my teenage years, the crime-solving exploits of Sherlock Holmes monopolised my reading time, as well as cheap love stories, in which the only physical contact between the hero and his virginal sweetheart was the touching of hands, before love culminated on the last page in a proposal of marriage and a happy-end kiss.

Today, prepubescent and teenage boys and girls would laugh at the unworldly pastimes of my childhood and adolescent years, maybe lighting another cigarette or passing around a 'joint', while poking fun at unheard-of attitudes, such as respect for parents and courtesy towards elders. How they would laugh at the idea of growing up in a social clime in which for most children of my time, babies were still delivered by stork, where virginity was expected in young brides, and the words promiscuity, eroticism and libido, as well as today's smutty terms for the sex act, were not yet part of our vocabulary and of as much interest to us as politics or the life cycle of the common housefly. When, eventually, our minds comprehended the physical union between a man and woman, it was something with which we did not concern ourselves unduly, subtle homilies by our elders, and the moralistic stance of German films, repeatedly reminding us that for a 'decent' girl such activity had to be confined to marriage.

As in those days women, particularly those brought up in middle-class families with a religious or strict moral code, were not expected to enjoy sex, such attitudes may, arguably, have sometimes promoted frigidity or made each marital coupling an open-eyed endurance test. Yet I ask myself whether in today's liberal sexual climate libido-freed, but romance-starved, women do not sometimes yearn for the days when woman was not so overtly portrayed as an 'object of lust'.

A victim of progress is undoubtedly the family. In the 'good old days', a structured family life provided stability. It taught discipline, values and aspirations. Marriage was the alpha and omega of parenthood. Today, the traditional family as a public institution and social unit is breaking up fast. Single-parent families are on the increase, and often enough homosexual partners are parenting a child. Critics see in the present trend not only the gradual destruction of the family as a nucleus, but also the seed to many ills of today's society. It is a development that arguably forms a parallel to the licentiousness and hedonistic lifestyle of the Romans, which led to the decline of the Roman empire.

A recollection of my school-days reveals the changes that have taken place in primary and secondary education since the beginning of the Thirties. In my first year at school, we still wrote with a graphite pencil on slates. I remember the rows of wooden desks with inkwells and, at secondary school level, the broad-spectrum curriculum consisting of twelve subjects, in eleven of which we had to take exams, including gymnastics and athletics, PT disciplines keenly promoted by Nazi educationalists.

While sex education in school would still have to wait another sixty years, it was the procreating behaviour of insects which in biology classes first tried to prepare the lower forms for the pairing of domestic animals and, ultimately, for the 'baby-making' procedure of married couples. Needless to say, our timorous teacher never made time in her syllabus to advance our knowledge. It was only by picking up the odd intimation from 'enlightened' class-mates that I began to suspect that there was more going on between parents than the occasional hug and kiss.

Classes in our girls-only school were small, and discipline was strict. Blessedly, our minds were not being confused by the barrage of information available today to youngsters on TV and in newspapers and magazines on sex. In needlework class we had to make a blouse, finish buttonholes and knit socks, lessons which I endured by thinking of the pleasures of going swimming, ice-skating or riding my bike after school. Despite my antipathy to such homecrafts, I learned at least how to use needle and thread to good effect, something that in our throwaway society cannot be said of many young women, who do not know how to mend a hole in a sock, arrest a run in tights or sew on a button.

School began at 8 am and ended at 1 or 2 o'clock in the afternoon. In summer, when temperatures soared above 28 °C,

'Hitzefrei' was announced, and to cries of delight, we would be skipping off to swimming-pools or the as yet unpolluted Havel river.

In our last year at school, attendance at private ballroom dancing classes was part of the finishing touches of our education. Under the stern eyes of the dancing mistress, and wearing our Sunday best, we would dance the foxtrot and quickstep with timid seventeen and eighteen year-old grammar school boys who would move around the parquet floor like wooden manikins. With the propriety of the time, physical contact between the dancers was restricted to a minimum.

On the downside, in the late Thirties and early Forties politically-oriented lessons were added to the curriculum, boring propaganda subjects which - judging by the lack of interest among my class-mates (apart from one devoted Hitler Youth maiden), did not appear to increase our political awareness, nor breed more Nazi disciples. But then this was Potsdam, the stronghold of Prussian aristocrats and a predominantly anti-fascist middle class.

In the Twenties and until the beginning of the war, life passed at a leisurely pace. Shopping had not yet become an obsession, and the frugality of life was still aeons away from today's consumerism. On Sundays, churches were full, and in cities families went for afternoon strolls along boulevards or took to the countryside with friends and picnic baskets. I remember my father being sartorially dressed for a promenade down the Kurfürstendamm or the Unter den Linden, wearing galoshes, a stiff-collar shirt, and a white handkerchief neatly folded in his breast pocket. My mother would look equally elegant in a modish outfit, and she would not be seen without a hat and gloves. I was no less handsomely attired: summer saw me in a pretty pink or sky-blue ruched frock with a matching bow in my hair, winter in a white woollen coat and hat. The crowning touch of such afternoon outings would be a visit to one of the all-gilt, marble and red plush boulevard cafés, where a luscious cream cake, and hot chocolate topped with a mound of whipped cream, spelled Arcadia.

It was still a '*heile Welt*'[1] for me, a world devoid of evil, greed and bloodshed, for the violent street clashes between communists and National Socialists in the early Thirties did not invade my childhood space. And whatever horrors I might pick up from the news still recoiled from my unsullied view of the world.

I am inclined to hail the good old days for the etiquette which still existed at the various social levels, and for some of the commendable customs which are noticeably disappearing in our fast-living, increasingly atheist and indulgent age. Society is certainly poorer for disregarding, or remaining ignorant of what once lent a certain grace to living. Today, all too few children know about social graces or are being taught the basics of good manners. But then the uncivilised behaviour of many parents in public and within their own family is all too often prevalent, and this, we know, easily corrupts their offspring.

When I was young, boys would bow, girls curtsey, when being introduced to or shaking the hand of an adult. We would not dare to shout at our parents or interrupt a conversation. Nor would we leave the table between courses or at the end of a meal, without asking for permission. Good table manners were also *de rigeur*. We did not poke the air with knives and forks, nor load our plates as if we had just finished a fast. Slurping would cause raised eyebrows. We were also taught to say 'please' and 'thank you', and to wash our hands before sitting down for a meal. We learned about respect for older people, and about the biblical interpretation of Sunday as a day of rest. We watched adults holding their wine glasses at the stem, and never saw people drinking straight from the bottle, as would now seem to be an accepted trend. We observed and copied what bestowed a certain grace to everyday behaviour. The

---

[1] sound world

41

cultivation of such decorum did not harm us, nor did it inhibit our development. Yet now that the death knell is ringing for the manners of the good old days, we of the old school have to live with what Allison O'Mara, author of The Best Times, describes as a hedonistic 'Me' generation. However, in all fairness, I should add that, thank goodness there is a growing number of young people nowadays who do not subscribe to a 'Me' codex and a 'to-hell-with-everybody-else' attitude. They, I believe, provide a hopeful altruistic counterbalance.

Nostalgia may cling to the days when for many people cars were neither an affordable or essential means of transport, nor a status symbol; when steam trains were running on time and trams rattling along city streets without polluting the air for pedestrians. We may yearn for an era when a functional family life and educational excellence prepared youngsters for the big world outside; when Godless Sunday shopping and the adverse effects of consumerism did not yet modify our lifestyle, and innocent people were not yet the target of psychopaths or members of a violent antisocial and cultural underclass, a time in which ultimately the Church, the law, schools and the nuclear family taught and upheld moral values.

Today our rural landscape is riddled with motorways; traffic and noise pollution in towns and cities are taking their human toll, while the temples of supermarkets and giant shopping complexes are drawing the life blood from small shops in towns and villages. Drugs and crime add to the rape of our quality of life. In its untainted way, it is only accessible today to the super rich, and to those who, equipped with the Bible or their own mantra, opt for a simple lifestyle away from the manipulative, addictive and soul-destroying ways of modern living.

But then again, who would want to live at a time when health and social services are still at an embryonic or pilot stage, child labour does not raise an eyebrow and infant mortality is high? When with industrial pollution unchecked, belching chimneys still deposit grime in people's lungs and medicine, as we know it today, is still in its infant shoes. Of course, the land would then be greener, lakes and streams be a haven for fish; the fields would be free of pesticides, and the threat of terrorism and a nuclear Armageddon still be a fantasy.

A bird's eye view of the past and present cannot ignore the educational and recreational merits of television, even if a surfeit of mindless shows provides entertainment for the less discerning, and cameras lovingly dwell on every football, dart and snooker ball. As for the glut of gratuitous violence and borderline pornography on screen, delivered to the viewer on a platter and arguably adding to some of the ills of our society, no one has to watch what offends the moral palate.

I would, however, applaud the means of modern communications, which not only bring global events to our TV screens, but have also shrunk the world to the time it takes to dial a number or send an e-mail message.

Food in our part of the world is no longer scarce. Yet I remember the humble, farm-reared chicken which used to be a Sunday or festive treat. Today it is part of our diet, as are many other food items sold in supermarkets, which thirty years ago would only have been available from special delicatessen shops or not have reached the consumer at all. Yet we did not have to worry about additives, preservatives, pesticides and genetically engineered food, not about such monsters as Salmonella, E. coli, Listeria and Creutzfeldt-Jakob disease. Honey, apples and cod-liver oil were panaceas, milk stood for healthy bones and daily PT classes in school for muscle power. Fast and pre-cooked, microwavable food had not yet replaced proper cooking in kitchens; burgers, pizzas, chips and ketchup were not yet the culinary preference of youngsters.

Looking at the advantages progress has brought to women, I can hear the outcry if the Pill were to be withdrawn, or fashion gurus were to prescribe the whalebone corset for their new slim-waist and pompous *derrière* fashion lines. Or if sex discrimination were still confining women to the nursery,

43

the kitchen and church pews. In Germany up to World War II, a woman's place was traditionally in what in the post-war and emerging feminist era was derisively labelled 'The Three K's': Kinder, Küche and Kirche. During the Hitler years, being a mother and housewife was being hailed as an honourable and nationally important role. Today, women would rebel if such party politics were denying them work places to which their education and career aspirations entitled them. I might add as an afterthought that perhaps many a husband might secretly wish today that a woman's place were still as narrowly staked as in the good old days.

Today our people have never had it so good, cry the ruling politicians. No one has to go hungry, major health care is still free and there are job vacancies or training schemes for those willing to work. The State is both father and mother to its subjects, even though, critics might add, it pretends to be blind and deaf in certain areas.

But now we who remember all too well, raise our hands. And don't let's forget, we say, that there has been peace in our part of the world for more than half a century.

As I picked up my pint of milk this morning, and the daily paper was delivered in time for my first mug of tea, I came to the conclusion that progress will always remain a double-edged sword. As the word implies, it will never be static. Forever flowing into some distant uncharted sea, we are being swept along, whether or not we long to swim back upstream for a mile or two. But then, we who have profited from the blessings of the good old days can always dream of them in old-fashioned nostalgia, before taking stock of what is good in our time.

2007

ANGST ERODES THE SOUL

Angst defines itself as irrational, yet tangible fear of something that may never happen or will, inevitably, at some point in our life. Angst feeds on reasoning and, once it grows elephantine, it will cripple our spirit and energy.

Believe me, I know. As an inveterate worrier - no doubt due to a flaw in my genetic makeup - I have been a victim of angst whenever the problems of old age, some conceivable painful experiences or seemingly insoluble difficulties were looming up on my life's horizon.

Angst comes in many disguises, and it is never more destructive than when we hare lying awake in the depths of the night - that middle stretch which Julian Barnes in Parenthesis calls 'the sewery hours, in which no light creeps through the curtains, and which allows venomous currents to run through our consciousness.' It is a time when our soul is most vulnerable and fear may be painting nightmarish scenarios. For what our eyes cannot actually see, our ears not hear and our bodies not feel, our angst-ridden imagination will perceive and magnify, often to elephantine proportions. During such Stygian journeys, common sense is left impotent.

Nearly 2000 years ago, Seneca, the Roman Stoic philosopher, statesman, diplomat and orator, who is best known for his thoughts on life and death, greed and money, saw angst as self-seeding and proliferating. In his letters to Lucilius on the subject of fear, he speaks of many things that may weigh heavily on our minds, and which cause us suffering because they exist more in our imagination than in reality. He advises his pupil not to be prematurely unhappy, as what we see as threatening may never happen.

For many of us, the fear of death and dying may be all too real. But to cope with our descent into old age and the final departure from this life, each of us has to find his own formula. Perhaps it is a human condition, to fear what we do not know, yet for those of us who allow angst to riot in their minds it is a tragedy.

The phenomenon of angst is suitably demonstrated in the Legend of Croquemitaine, in which a castle symbolises irrational fear and the many terrible obstacles that such fear may conjure up. The hypothetical Fear-Fortress is said to vanish into thin air, if it is approached with a brave heart and a clear conscience.

> 'It sunk before my earnest face,
> It vanished quite a way,
> Between me and the day
> Such castles rise to strike the dumb;
> But weak in every part,
> They melt before a strong man's eyes
> And fly the true of heart.'

Aeschylus called fear 'stronger than arms'. Equally valid is Edmund Burke's assessment of it in Philosophical Surgery Into the Origin of the Sublime and Beautiful. He maintains that no passion so effectively robs the mind of all its powers of acting and reasoning than fear.

Even Don Quixote ruminated over the philosophy of fear. For him it was sharp-sighted, seeing underground and high up in the skies. Indeed, sharp-sightedness is arguably one of the features of angst - the tendency to see things that may be no more than bogies and, at best, are grossly distorted. In the same vein, Boris Pasternak speaks of fear having the largest eyes of all.

Sound reasoning thus tells me that the only thing we have to fear is angst itself - the wild excesses of the imagination, the often groundless terror that paralyses us; the very chimera that devours our souls and in the process, often breaks down the body's defences.

For those afflicted by angst, whether in the wakeful hours of the night or beneath daylight shadows, its predatory effects may be thwarted - by thinking of the allegorical castle. Others may find that a busy lifestyle or something pleasant to look forward to will keep the intruder at bay. Christians, on the other hand, may take courage in prayer or in Psalm 91:5: 'Thou shalt not be afraid for the terror by night; nor for the arrow that flieth by day'. There is no panacea for fighting the virus angst, other than by the above means, if not by viewing rationally whatever is assuming a threatening shape. After all, what we expect may never materialise, while what is inescapable will - because it is so written.

'Angst frisst die Seele auf' - was the title of a German film in the late Seventies. Apparently I was not mature enough to take the lesson it imparted to heart. I did not see angst for what it was: the monster which gobbles up the soul of those who cross the proverbial bridge before they come to it. Or for whom the inescapable, the seemingly insoluble or grossly disproportionate creates images of terror. It took me a long time to realise that once across that bridge we often find the grass greener, paths smoother and the sun shining brighter. Phantoms will no longer scare from beyond. The Castle of Croquemitaine will have vanished.

At a critical stage of my life, I wrote the following poem, in which angst is in turn a whip, an apocalyptic rider, a faceless serpentine being and an invader:

LYING AWAKE AT NIGHT

It gallops towards you,
its hooves clattering
on the cobblestones
of wakefulness, its whip
cracking the silence
of the sleepless night

It rattles on windows
forcing its entry,
seeps through the crevices
of the naked mind, assaults
with images as scary
as a Kafkaesque dream.

It creeps from cupboards,
uncoils from corners
multiplies and grows
into new, black entities
advances, devours you
before the light of dawn.

47

While fear in its positive form activates our survival instinct, angst with its negative connotations disables us. As such, it also features widely in poetry, legends and aphorisms. What such writings teach us is that angst is counteractive. It is also a waste of energy and a waste of living. And living the present to the full is what we ought to concentrate on, so declares not only my inner voice, but common sense. I might be slow in learning to banish angst from my life, but the signs are good. One day I shall be able to face the future, the inevitable and those distant bridges with equanimity.

2007

CLOUDS

One spring morning, shortly after sunrise, I stood at my window, looking out across the garden to the rising meadows beyond, which were dotted with sheep and new-born lambs. In the distance, standing out sharply against the skyline, a herd of cattle was moving along in single file. Not a leaf stirred. My mind was a blank, my whole being was rejoicing with the promise of a fine day. Then I saw it: a feather-like, faintly rose-tinted cloud, often referred to as a 'mare's tail'. It was floating high over the awakening pastoral scene.

Clouds do not make headlines. Few of us give them a second glance unless we are getting ready for a barbecue, a children's *al fresco* birthday party or some sporting event. At harvest time farmers may smile at a sunny open sky or utter expletives at the sight of approaching rain clouds that pledge more than a few drops of rain. Ominous cloud formations seldom cause the cancellation of athletic events: golfers, with their eyes on their tee-off stance, the distant green and the birdie potential of the next hole, have no time to assess the potential behaviour of clouds. Serious cloud spotters will also seldom be found in inner cities or built-up areas, where high buildings and narrow streets leave but mean patches of sky, nor will commuters have the time or urge to cloud-watch. Serious aficionados will seek a wide-screen or hilly countryside.

In some people of an oversensitive disposition, the sight of storm-brewing clouds allegedly induces moments of subliminal fear. Yet landscape artists would be lost without clouds on canvas to suit the theme of their composition, while ramblers - with one professional look at the sky - will take along either a sun hat or appropriate rain gear.

In times of draught, water companies give rain-promising clouds the thumbs-up, welcoming a good cloudburst to replenish low water tables and reservoirs; gardeners will rub their hands at the prospect of rain quenching the thirst of their flower beds and vegetable plots. And, as we greet soil-drenching, cleansing rain, we may realise how in hot climes people strain their eyes for rain clouds.

Although no more than visible condensed water vapour, the simple cloud has given rise to many quotations throughout the ages. The earliest observation comes from a 14th century monk who declared that 'between a man and God there is not a cloud or air, but The Cloud of Unknown' - a term paraphrased by Malcolm Muggeridge in A Spiritual Journey as 'The Cloud of Unknowing'; a theme to which John Polkinghorne also refers in Faith In God In An Age Of Science. In his opera *Der Freischütz*, Karl Maria von Weber proclaims that even if hidden by a cloud, the sun will remain in the sky *('...und ob die Wolke sie verhülle, die Sonne bleibt am Himmel')*. Shakespeare in Henry VI states that 'every cloud does not engender a storm'. Similarly, and by now a well-worn cliché, we speak of every cloud having 'a silver lining'.

And what about English poetry? Here, clouds often present heart-warming images. What better time then than to look up and read relevant passages when the sky has a washed-out look, mist is shrouding familiar contours and we are feeling solidly earth-bound; what better tonic for our morale than to wander with Wordsworth 'lonely as a cloud/that floats on o'er hills and vales', or to watch with Keats 'how clouds bloom the soft-dying day and the stubble-plains with a rosy hue'?

Nor have clouds escaped romantic negative connotations. 'To live in the cloud' means to live in dreamland, a place removed from reality like Thomas More's Utopia. Wine that is clouded either points to poor quality bottling, deficient corkage or faulty storage. Personal problems may also build up like miasmic clouds, just as excess of alcohol or mind-changing substances will stupefy, mock or falsely prettify reality.

Clouds come well-assorted. They may be bulbous or fleecy, look like ribbons or straying lambs, and in ominous formation resemble an army ready for battle. Whatever their colour, design or density, they have their devoted 'spotters' and 'analysts'. One of them is a German cousin of mine, who once visited me in Scotland. Proud of my Scottish residency at the time, I took her sightseeing to the Western Highlands - through the breathtaking beauty of mountains, glens and heather-clad vales, along mirror-like lochs and bubbling streams. But whatever dramatic views were lying before us, all she admired were the clouds above. She would, indeed, wax lyrical about every pristine, white convex structure seemingly stacked on top of each other and, here and there, ballooning, bulking sideways without obfuscating the sun or stealing the silver gleam off a loch's smooth table of water. In child-like admiration she used superlatives and, later in Glasgow, raided every touristy postcard stack for pictures of 'Scottish' clouds. 'They don't come like that at home', she said.

Clouds may sometimes mock genuine theatre. As if it were yesterday I recall a strange experience on board a cruise ship anchored about a mile or two off Syracuse harbour.

Launches were shuttling passengers back to ship at the end of individual land-going stints, when I noticed - in an otherwise amicable sky - a black, opaque cloud-bed hovering low over the ship, its edges well-defined: like some evil emanation. Like a satanic tongue. My imagination went into overdrive. It conjured up images of some extraterrestrial substance about to descend and choke or suck up the ship - the perfect opening for a science fiction story. I admit that I was not only utterly puzzled, but also momentarily overcome by a feeling of unease. Yet none of the odd passengers on deck, who were reading or dozing, nor any passing member of the crew, seemed to have noticed this singular, eerie spectacle which was draining the ship of sunlight. Luckily, I had my camera at hand, to witness what was just short of touching the ship's funnel. Minutes later, the mass overhead moved on, quickly thinning out, soaking up sunlight and finally drifting away in a white haze like a bride's veil. To this day no one has been able to explain this phenomenon to me. However, my photographs prove that I did not proverbially 'have my head in the clouds' at the time.

Having cruised through the Atlantic, the Mediterranean and the Arctic Ocean, and sailed through the ill-famed waters of the Bay of Biscay, the monsoon-ridden Indian Ocean and the South China Sea, I have seen the kind of cloudscapes which Russia's best-known Romantic artist, Aivazovsky, painted so brilliantly: clouds crossing the paths of the sun or moon, boiling over a tempestuous sea or drifting solo over calm waters, the kind of clouds that will either colour the sea an anaemic grey or nightmarish black, or - if stuck up high in the atmosphere - will not tone down the silver fleece on a sun- or moon-lit ocean.

Today, on a damp, grizzly November morning, a thick cloud cover hovers over the land, not allowing the sun even to streak through. The rain-saturated air, which reeks of decaying leaves, warns of similar days to come, before winter makes its entrance. A melancholic day. A day to keep one's eyes on the ground, while inveterate cloud-watchers can only dream of Cumulus, Cirrus, Nimbus and Mare's Tails, or of that lonely cloud that 'floats high o'er hills and vales...'.

But then we know that even the most leaden sky will eventually pale and invite the sun back, before another cloudscape will delight its avid observers.

2006

52

STRICTLY CONFIDENTIAL

'Facts, facts, facts, is all you need', declares Mr Gradgrind in
Hard Times. For some this may be an arguable maxim, but a
few facts will have to precede this story nonetheless. They will
explain how my mother ended up first in the Berlin Air
Ministry, then in its secret WWII operational headquarters;
how after the war she came to work in the murky corridors of
the Gehlen Intelligence Organisation, the agency run by
General Gehlen, Germany's legendary spymaster, and which
later formed part of Federal Germany's Intelligence Service,
the *Bundesnachrichtendienst* or BND. In close co-operation
with Allied intelligence agencies, notably the CIA and MI5,
this was gathering information on Communist East Germany
and the USSR's military power in the build-up to the Cold
War. Facts will also explain how - due to the 'Top Secret'
nature of her work - however subordinate her position had
been, she would remain bound by Official Secrets Acts until
the two countries' reunification.

It all started when my parents got divorced in 1936.
Under Nazi policy divorces were frowned upon, and it was
difficult to obtain a Decree Absolute as Hitler saw the German
family as a 'wholesome', indivisible union - the backbone of
the Reich. Having filed for divorce on the grounds of
incompatibility, my mother was desperate. Forced by the
Court's deliberate procrastination, and finding herself in an
untenable domestic position, she agreed to plead the guilty
party, in order to secure a Final Decree. Yet fabricated though
such admission was, it made her pay a high price. For her plea
absolved my father from paying alimony. However, the Court
made him - a high earner in those days - responsible for
financing my upbringing and education.

Penniless, my mother now moved in with my
grandmother who had lost most of her considerable financial

assets in the Wall Street Crash, and who had since found it difficult to cope with a down-sized lifestyle which allegedly was affecting her health. My father, in what he must have reckoned to provide a more stable environment, thus placed me into a private children's home in Potsdam, where I was to attend a fee-paying high school for girls. It was a relocation which would have a far-reaching effect on my life. I never asked the reason for such a drastic change. In those days, ten year-olds just did not question parental decisions.

Staring reality in the face, facts now forced my mother to earn a living. To find a job. To rub shoulders with commuters. Having married early and reigned supremely as a housewife and dinner hostess (albeit assisted by a live-in maid), she was the proverbial *'Tochter aus gutem Haus'*, well brought-up and educated to master the social graces of her class. She had graduated from a finishing school, learning to make polite conversation in French, dance gracefully to ballroom tunes and practise the type of homecraft which included care of household linen, a knowledge of wines and fine cuisine. She played Schumann beautifully on the piano and enjoyed opera, philharmonic concerts and the theatre. She also dressed with understated elegance and, for a stroll down Berlin's famous boulevards or a visit to one of its elegant turn-of-the-century coffee-houses, she would don a hat, white gloves and the inevitable row of pearls. She had read Tolstoy's Anna Karenina, and on her bookshelf stood works by Galsworthy, Wiechert, Goethe and Rilke.

However, circumstances often breed their own rules. Indeed, they are often the genesis of a person's survival spirit. My mother thus discovered that she was made of sterner stuff. She took classes in shorthand and typing, and in 1938 found a job in the Berlin Air Ministry as secretary to a senior Air Force officer, an appointment which required her to sign the Official Secrets Act. I don't know what kind of sensitive information became part of her working life, but so shortly before

Germany's invasion of Poland, and the build-up of the German *Luftwaffe* in the overture to the Second World War, she would have been privy to many 'Top Secret' memoranda.

All went well, she told me, until her boss groped under her skirt one day, suggesting a quick romp behind the filing cabinet. Perhaps he thought that a pretty widow was easy game, perhaps even asking for it, however demure and straight-laced her appearance.

Shocked into a world she had only read about, my mother immediately handed in her notice which due to the nature of the work was not accepted. Instead, without giving her an option, she was transferred to the secret operation headquarters in the Wildpark forest near Potsdam - a mini underground city of control rooms and staff living quarters. By now, WWII had been declared and the campaign for Hitler's expansion policies was in full swing. In Wildpark HQ, working in shifts around the clock, staff were allowed no more than one free weekend a month. Not surprisingly, in such an enforced, unnatural environment, bereft of sunlight and fresh air, my mother developed tuberculosis which confined her to a sanatorium for six months. Subsequently released from her job, and enjoying an all too brief period as a newly-wed, she was to live out the remaining chaotic years of the war under circumstances that severely tested her survival spirit.

After the war, and with life in the bomb-ravaged capital assuming a modicum of normality, she once again found herself in dire need of a supplement to her income. She applied to an advertisement seeking a 'mature, trustworthy lady' as secretary to the manager of an insurance company. My mother had never heard of the company before but so soon after the war, many new enterprises were emerging from the country's economic ruins. What, however, startled her in the advertiser's reply was that he insisted on conducting the interview at her home, an unconventional request which even in today's society would raise a candidate's eyebrows. As the job came with an attractive salary, my mother had no alternative but to invite the gentleman to her house, no doubt feeling safe in the knowledge that I was staying with her at the time.

On the day of the interview I opened the door to a man of middle age, about whom everything was of an unrelieved grey, except his steel-blue eyes which betrayed an intelligence of the highest order. A well-guarded smile rushed across his face. 'Schmidt is the name,' he said, 'I've come to see Frau Börner.'

I was asked to leave the room. Yet, although I stayed with my ear close to the door, I was unable to overhear a single word of the hushed conversation.

Well, my mother got the job. Due to her previous, though merely clerical involvement with highly confidential matters, the job must have fitted her like a glove. Many years later I learned that she had to sign a new Official Secrets Act and thus become a tiny cog in Cold War Western intelligence operations which shared information with MI5 and the CIA. I also gathered from my mother's description that Herr Schmidt's 'Insurance' office was located in one of the back rooms of a grocer's store, an obviously ideal camouflage for clandestine operations. Smiley would have loved the place, as informants could enter it like shoppers and come out with a pound or two of goods without raising the suspicion of any East German agent. The Gehlen Intelligence Service thus had a classic spyhole in the city's Western sector.

In 1963 the Gehlen Organisation became Federal Germany's *Bundesnachrichtendienst* (BND), which would have restructured Western intelligence and counter-intelligence services. I don't know when my mother left, and whether it was of her own free will or by being made redundant. Yet - despite her minor role - she was certainly 'blacklisted' by DDR and Russian espionage agencies. And like most members and former members of 'sensitive' Western agencies, she was not allowed to go into East Berlin or cross the DDR zone by train, to visit friends or relatives. The German Federal Government would pay for a return flight every time until the Wall went down in 1989.

The fact remains that my gentle, oh so socially and culturally refined mother was neither a Mata Hari nor a female operative employed by a Circus of John le Carré fame. Small fry though she may have been in the notorious Cold War intelligence game, a whiff of secrecy would hang about her for some time to come. No wonder that the term 'Strictly Confidential' took on a new meaning for me.

2008

MOVING HOUSE LATE IN LIFE

Moving house, they say, causes stress secondary only to bereavement and divorce. The effect of changing one's abode late in life in particular, cannot be measured on a Richter scale, but like an earthquake it will vary in intensity, depending on the age, adaptability and inner readiness of the individual.

How traumatic then is the uprooting of the elderly, for whom health reasons or lack of back-up social services dictate a change of residence, whether a move into sheltered accommodation or a resettlement closer to their families.

This is where an acute sense of loss becomes tangible. Suddenly, the familiar views from the windows have gone, and some of the little things which matter to us, and which so easily grow into a beloved routine, are erased by a move to a new environment.

How elderly people cope with the initial disorientation and the ensuing relocation is, essentially, a question of mental attitude and the will to cope. Once in their new residence, nothing will serve them worse than piling up nostalgia for the home they left behind. Instead of looking back, all efforts should be geared to making the new home another castle, the new environment the accepted backdrop to living.

I know what it takes. A few years ago I moved from Scotland to a Kentish village, prompted by health reasons and the commendable wish of my eldest doctor son and his family to have me within easy reach.

I never regretted the decision.

At the age of seventy-one it was by no means an easy feat to sever my roots and move to new pastures. By doing so I closed one chapter of my life and opened a new one. For me, it also posed a challenge. I was leaving behind a much-loved house and garden, and some close friends. The loss of the latter is the most tangible, for a distance of several hundred miles is a true divider, and no telephone calls, no letter-writing can retain the immediacy and potency of such friendships. And old folk know how difficult, if not impossible, it is to make real friends late in life, people with whom one can bond, and with whom one either shares mutual experiences or has something else in common.

I was fortunate in that my state of health did not advocate a move into sheltered accommodation and that I had the necessary finance to choose a new house which satisfied my requirements. Many people in my position do not have that option.

In the upheaval of moving and resettling, I was helped by my philosophy which commands me always to make the best of any given situation, to find a speedy solution to any problems and, whenever facing major decisions, carefully to look at figures, acknowledge personal needs and listen to my inner voice. The house I finally settled for was one which had the potential to become a home, the kind where sleep comes easily at night; where the view from windows lifts the spirit even on a bleak day and provides a happy hunting ground for creative thoughts. Where, ultimately, the garden could be turned into a green and blossoming spa for the soul.

While I was still living out of a suitcase in my son's house, I wrote the following poem which reflects my sentiments at the time:

Departure

For the last time
I walk through rooms
that now are no more
than empty shells,
naked, but for the memories
they hold.
I lock the door behind me,
slowly, as one shuts a book
which has earned its place
on one's shelf.
A blank page stares at me,
and all I know is
that a chapter of my life
has ended.

An ache rises inside me,
as I walk through the garden
reared over the years
in loving toil.
A last look at the roses,
the cherry tree, at plants
voicing their farewell
in plaintive silence.
The parting sun erases
the familiar horizon,
and all I know is
that a chapter of my life
has ended.

I do not look back,
allowing images to fade,
to make room, somewhere,
for new companions.
A cold wind hugs me,
then drives its fist
into my back,
urging me forward.
A neighbour waves
from the window,
and all I know is
that a new chapter of my life
waits to be written.

1998

THE TUNNELS

In the Going-Back game, one experience stands out in my mind: the return visit to the famous tunnels of Gibraltar's Rock. It was prompted perhaps more by curiosity than a perverse wish to recall a nightmarish midnight hour in 1961, when fear for the life of my eldest son, and the threat of an emergency flight to a London hospital, had turned me into a humble mendicant.

I was on a Mediterranean cruise a few years ago, when my ship first berthed at Gibraltar for a few hours. Passengers were given the option either to go on a conducted tour up the Rock, to meet the cheeky, free-roaming Barbary apes - the only native species of apes in Europe - or to visit the equally famous WWII maze of tunnels that are sneaking through the mighty limestone Rock known to classical scholars as one of the pillars of Hercules. I opted for a tour through the tunnels, although my fellow trippers were all male and old soldiers mainly interested in the Rock's wartime history. As the only woman among them, they good-humouredly enrolled me into their midst. They did not know that I had been there before. For a harrowing hour in 1961. And now I wanted to step back into the past, just as if a tourist I were revisiting an architectural or natural wonder of the world. What would I find?

The tour of the tunnels came with a guide who introduced himself in excellent English as a Gibraltarian of Moroccan-Maltese parentage. He briefly lectured us on the history of the tunnels, on which work had started in 1782 - the time of the Great Siege - using crowbar, hammer and gunpowder. In 1941 the threat of invasion by enemy forces had set off major work which turned the Rock into a fortress.

'The tunnels have only been open to the public since 2005', he said. 'They used to have their own power station and hospital.' I know, I know, I wanted to shout.

We walked gingerly through the draughty corridors which were lit by single low wattage naked bulbs and assailed the visitor with their dungeon-like, claustrophobic atmosphere. I was shivering, as strategically-placed wind machines blasted fresh air into the network.

'They also had accommodation for a thousand troops and civilians,' the guide continued.

By now I was staggering along, the last member of the human chain, fearing that I might get left behind and find myself lost in the creepy maze. Not too soon for me, the guide pointed to a steel door. 'This was the entrance to the hospital. It came complete with full diagnostic and laboratory facilities. Here doctors treated not only injured or battle-fatigued soldiers, but also local civilians.'

I know, I thought. I know. And like a film reeled off at high speed, the past sped back...

On his MoD posting to Hong Kong with his family, my husband had opted for the leisurely travel by sea on a small cargo boat, which would give us a once-in-a-lifetime chance to go ashore in several eastern ports not visited by large passenger ships. We had just settled down for the long journey, when halfway between Gibraltar and Malta, our eldest son, aged four, fell down to the lower deck through a gate carelessly left open by a member of the crew. The ship's doctor, whose breath - whatever time of day - was laced heavily with alcohol, was baffled by the child's sudden rise in temperature. He suspected a cranial fracture that could have upset the temperature-regulating centre of the brain, and prescribed an aspirin. He duly reported the incident to the captain who, after consultation with his shipping line, turned the ship around and sailed back to Gibraltar for the more modern diagnostic facilities of the Rock's British Army & Navy Hospital.

It was midnight when we arrived. In line with international regulations, whenever a passenger suffers from an infectious or suspect illness, the ship dropped anchor offshore and a launch took the child and myself to a waiting ambulance which soon threaded its way through the bowels of the Rock to the hospital wing. Here, three consultants and a pathologist were waiting for us in dinner jackets, having been called away from a party. The steel door closed behind them and their young patient, and I sat down on a stone bench in the chilly, dimly-lit and breezy corridor, waiting, waiting, whilst my mind painted the worst scenario…

As by now I formed the tail end of the group, I stopped for a few moments and stared at the door which was bolted and looked like silver that had not been cleaned for years. But where was the bench on which I had been waiting and worrying that night, whilst feeling the chill of the tunnels creeping under my skin? The bench had gone; I was left with the sight of the aged door and ghostly images.

The Guide: 'Come on, folks. Stay close now.'

'You alright, lady?' someone asked me. I answered in the affirmative and quickened my steps. Like a celluloid ribbon, my memories had snapped. We soon squeezed through a narrow opening to emerge at a crossing of several tunnels which - so the guide said - had led to military HQ areas. He did not mention that should any visitors be left behind, they might feel utterly lost as to which corridor led to the way out. Not surprisingly, and perhaps experiencing a whiff of unease, everybody now stayed close together. Then, at last, the Exit. Sunlight. Fresh air. The year 2007. As we climbed aboard the waiting coach, I realised that my visit to the tunnels and its former hospital had not served any purpose other than stirring up a flutter of gratitude: that, at the time, supplied with antibiotics and with his arm up to the elbow in plaster, our son had been declared well enough to return to the ship and continue the sea journey with his family.

He had - most likely in the week before embarkation - contracted glandular fever and, due to the accident on ship, a green-stick fracture of his wrist. The ship's doctor was dismissed at the end of the voyage for his gross misdiagnosis which had cost the shipping company twenty-four hours of sailing time. Keeping a low profile, he would not speak to us again for the rest of the passage.

2008

COME, FLY WITH ME

According to a *Times* article, and an editorial which could have been written by A A Gill or Jeremy Clarkson (known for their wit, critical vein and use of extended metaphors), the luggage of one in thirty of British Airways passengers is likely to go AWOL these days.

Now, the army of BA travellers may ask, how can a locked suitcase, flight-numbered and destination-labelled, get lost, either never to be seen again or with one's beachwear flying to Anchorage and one's business suit or black tie gear ending up in some outpost of civilisation? Or, as in some cases, to be reunited weeks later with its owner, locks miraculously still intact.

Where, or with whom, lies the blame? Do check-in labels perhaps come off in transit due to the airline using a cheaper brand of glue, in order to save a penny or two? Is airport luggage transfer perhaps unable to cope at certain times due to the sheer volume of baggage to be moved? Or have handlers, like their colleagues worldwide, developed a system that allows them to make a desirable suitcase 'disappear' without a trace? Would 'Big Brother' surveillance cameras, strung around luggage loading and retrieval areas, perhaps act as a plain-clothes policeman, likely to catch *in flagrante* a single operator or bag-thieving gang?

Nowadays air travellers require physical and mental stamina. They also need a reservoir of patience, when facing delays, over-booking, control-tower computer hitches or cancellations. Vocal restraint is also recommended when realising that one's suitcase has not made it to beach resort, conference centre or granny's eightieth, and that - apart from Andalusian, Fifth Avenue or Hong Kong shopping items - all these souvenirs may never see the owner's mantelpiece.

Long check-in queues for popular flights, frequent terminal chaos, and toilets which by midday resemble the

WC's of Third World facilities, have also made air travel an onus. Moreover, once we are through the various anti-terrorist checkpoints, having declared the absence of nail scissors, liquids, and kitchen knives, we should be able to relax in departure lounges, reading or using our laptop.

But not a chance! For our thoughts are now gyrating around the all-important question: will my suitcase turn up at the baggage reclaim carousel or not? And what if it doesn't? The tension resulting from painting a negative scenario is likely to create that hollow feeling we experience when waiting at the dentist's for root treatment or tooth extraction.

'Come, fly with me', intones BA, allegedly the worst loser of baggage. And we do, teeth grinding. Because island-bound as we are, we cannot walk or drive across the Atlantic or other far-flung places, nor make it to the Continent by horse, trap, camel or on foot. Some travellers, still reeling from a previous loss or misdirected luggage, may now motor to the Channel Tunnel, others may prefer ferry services. But hey, a new method of cross-Channel transport may soon be on the drawing-board. Last week, Yves Rossie - now named 'The Rocket Man' - made history by flying with one jet-propelled wing from the French coast to the White Cliffs of Dover and back at 125 mph. According to observers, he did so with the lightness and grace of an eagle. Perhaps an Alan Sugar type of entrepreneur ought to take the French pilot cum inventor under his business wings and encourage him to develop a load-bearing, multi jet-propelled system that would allow disillusioned BA and other air passengers to take them and their luggage abroad - nail scissors, pen knife and all.

So over to you, Monsieur Rossie!

2008

MANY A SWEET SONG TO SING

Once upon a time - and this is not a fairy story - retirement still had a clearly definable, though often less rigid upward boundary. Older people were still valued for their work ethic and experience. These days, due to global economic recession, many men and women who are still light years away from legal or optional retirement are given the not-so-friendly boot by cash-strapped companies. Suddenly finding themselves in the palpable void of unemployment, angry, their life not only financially derailed, they have little in common with the retirees of the Seventies and Eighties.

Then, when retirement beckoned, it was welcomed after a full working life. Sweet was the thought of no longer having to struggle out of bed in the morning, to catch the 7.10 train or whatever commuter routine a job required. Assuming the new pensioners had prudently managed their finances over the years, there now lay many options before them. Those who still had fire in their minds and vigour in their limbs would have rejected, *a priori*, a life of slippers, day-time television and boredom-intensive activities which are now considered to be a curtain-raiser to early dementia. Life at the hearth, they might say, was not for them - not yet. For there was still many a sweet song to sing.

Inevitably, though, the first pension slip might have invited thoughts about old age and an examination of beliefs, while plans for the future were already on the drawing board.

Today, many of us who have reached pensionable age or have been made redundant in mid-life, are bound to have one thing in common: a sudden acute awareness of growing old. Resignedly, or with pangs of regret, we see how our life is inexorably losing momentum like a toddler's spin-top. To make matters worse, our joints may be playing up, our memory begin to play tricks on us, our heart send out early warning messages. Our once youthful, determined stride may well by now have lost out to a stick-assisted slower gait, and when we look into the mirror, we are painfully aware of greying and thinning locks, and of those cruel lines which mark the passage of time - lines which often tell the tale of a life lived unwisely or unfavoured by the gods.

Yet we will have to accept the diverse crutches of old age; we may require glasses, a hearing aid, a walking stick. One day we will have arrived at what Shakespeare calls 'the Seventh Age', the years 'sans teeth, sans eyes, sans taste, sans everything'.

Yet the limitations of earlier centuries encountered by septuagenarians no longer hold true, for even when we are only a step away from patrician age, our final season need not be a mean one. We may no longer be roving Don Juans or *femmes fatales*, nor solid citizens able to move mountains or desirous of doing so. But many of us are now loving grandparents, living in the affection and in the light of our families - invaluable dividends for old age, and sadly denied to some old folk who find themselves living in the emotional and physical penumbra of lone widowhood.

Nevertheless, there is no getting away from it, let's face it: we have grown old.

Ah, but here is the rub. We may not feel as if we are approaching the gate to Nemesis, but we are officially classed as OAPs, entitled to concessions and a *soupçon* of indulgence. If we are lucky, some kind soul may give up his seat or hold open a door for us. We are not happy, though, if stand-up comedians and flippant youths call us the 'grey-haired brigade', a summary term which we think carries a whiff of denigration. The young, alienated hordes may at best tolerate us, at worst treat us with an overt lack of respect, call us unflattering names in their lingo or find pensioners an easy mugging prey. To them we are parasites on the taxpayer and an unsightly ballast on the NHS - we, the oldies who are still standing proudly for all the values of which the young are widely ignorant or dismissive, and which their gang ethics has declared 'uncool'.

Yet, while holding on to our lifeline, willing to have our acumen and personal commitment challenged, and making use of whatever mobility and mental agility the years have left us, new doors are opening. Never have gardening societies, bridge and bowls clubs, Women's Institutes, literary and music circles, as well as other groups with eclectic or creative interests, prospered more than today. In line with *chaçun à son goût*, football fans of advanced years can still reap the excitement they crave, live on screen, golfers try and reduce their handicaps with an eye on the hole-in-one. Other hobbyists may celebrate their wealth of leisure in their garden, workshop or shed, at a typewriter or computer, behind an easel or with a fishing rod. Keen walkers may be found on nature trails and bird-watchers on the lookout for some avian specimen. And not only do we now have more time for books, music and perhaps, religion, but we may become crossword and bridge routineers, join a choir, take up bee-keeping or painting, or start on that book which has been waiting to be written for decades. We also tend to become more selective in choosing new friends, and we may distance ourselves, or dismiss from our lives, people who no longer touch our orbit. Ultimately, we may cultivate a new-found charitable streak in our social fabric, while those among us, who have worked on their spiritual image, may now enjoy inner peace and tranquillity.

Living in an age in which education is not limited to young people, it is gratifying to know that for the not-so-young or not-yet-too-old opportunities for further study abound. Ever-greedy brains may opt for classes ranging from aesthetic philosophy to the culture of Ancient Greece, from Russian or Arabic to the study of Islam or Florentine art. Such educational pastimes are bound to add purpose and contentment to the days which, while seemingly getting shorter, suddenly have prime time added.

Blessedly, there are also some whimsical substitutes for the detractions of old age. We can now wear what we like, without kowtowing to fashion moguls. We may even don something outrageous, like a red hat with paper flowers or a George Melly jacket, without raising more than an eyebrow or an indulgent smile. (I would draw the line, though, at rebellious old men wearing washed-out jeans, logo-embellished T-shirts with baseball caps back to front, and, at dress size 22, women wearing shorts or skimpy dresses revealing bare, beefy legs.) No longer pricing our public image above everything, some of us may tend to be more outspoken, bluntly expressing our opinions, outmoded or didactic as they may well be; others may positively revel in eccentric behaviour. But then, all things considered, having reached our terminal age, we should be entitled to some foibles.

In our seventies, sometimes in our late sixties, we find that our awareness of life is undergoing a change. By necessity or a law of nature our perspectives are shifting, as are our priorities. Most of us who are finding ourselves on the downward slide of life are inclined to grow fiercely protective of our environment. As knights used to build fortified castles, to defend themselves against the enemy, so we buttress the walls of our shrunken universe against anything that may make a chink in them. Safe within such a bulwark we find peace or at least a modicum of serenity, perhaps boosted by a manageable, enjoyable daily routine: so we cope, or cope better, with the slings and arrows of old age, while living out the remaining years of our lives in a manner commensurate with our physical and mental energy.

Mind you, if we have never understood Einstein's $e=mc^2$ equation, we are unlikely to work it out now, whilst trying to remember some people's names may require a major brain search. Former devotees of rock and roll may now hum Gilbert & Sullivan tunes in the bath, lend their baritone voices to hymns or to the local choir, and with gusto join the Last Night of the Proms audience in the rendition of Rule Britannia.

Having missed out on the under-thirty club scene with its mental and physical surrender to disco dancing, and having no ear for hell-bending pop, acid rock or whatever frenzied sound now passes for 'music', many members of the older generation will still enjoy the pleasure of a ballroom waltz, while finding life more bearable when listening to the strains of the Forties and Fifties, or to classical and operatic fare.

Alas, old age is not just creaking joints, nostalgia and frequent catnaps. It often commands a brave effort to cope with ill health or increasing isolation; it may require pluck to look ahead, to balance one's books and deal with the nitty-gritty problems of everyday life. How easy it sounds. How hard it sometimes is, to soldier on and acknowledge that life compensates us in many small ways for what it takes away from us.

Indeed, happy are those of advanced age who, facing Tennyson's 'dying of the light', can look back on their life without major regrets or feelings of guilt, but safe in the knowledge of having achieved whatever lay within the boundaries of their capability and ambitions. Happy indeed are those who live to see their own Christian and moral standards being practised by their children and even passed on to their grandchildren, and who, although in sight of the ultimate frontier, are able to say:

> Gratefully, I pick up
> Every crumb of happiness,
> Every grain of fresh insight;
> Gracefully, I acknowledge
> The variegated messages
> Of Life's eventide;
> Humbly, I continue my search
> For the Unknowable.
>
> Yet though the days
> Seem to be flitting by
> With undue haste,
> I know I still have
> Many a drum to beat,
> MANY A SWEET SONG TO SING.

2000

THE SCREAM

I looked at it. It held me in a macabre thrall. Perhaps because I was so close to it in the Gallery, a mere metre or two. Perhaps because I had never been responsive enough in the past, having seen it only as an art-book lithograph.

Standing in front of Edvard Munch's The Scream, I could not help thinking of people who had never found themselves at the nadir of their life, never experienced moments of abysmal misery, the kind that makes a person utter a silent scream, a sound-proof, animal-like howl. Are they the lucky ones, the darlings of the gods? Does a fortuitous immunity from suffering make such people more receptive, more sympathetic towards the afflictions of others? Not having staggered through a private hell themselves, are they able to empathise and feel compassion for those who are crying out for help? Or does a life free of care and anguish conveniently blunt their sensitivity?

For the artist Tracey Emin, The Scream is suffused with a strong sense of loneliness. For her, it symbolises a human plight that dwells heavily upon the soul, behaves like a tidal wave crashing, drowning.

Yet in such a frozen landscape of existence, often no more is needed than an opportunity to unburden oneself to a patient and sympathetic listener. And what healing power lies in a hug and the comforting grip of a hand. How easily can a sufferer's sight often be directed towards that proverbial silver lining, how easily his perspective be re-aligned.

Alas, nowadays not many of us have the time, patience and an inner readiness, to act as a good Samaritan, and few of us possess the magical quality or the power needed to turn a silent scream into a smile. Those who have are surely blessed with a special humanity, one frequently boosted by faith, emotional stamina or an empirical 'I have been there' philosophy. For it does indeed require a special calibre of person to guide another through an episode in his life, in which everything that had so far provided crutches, suddenly appears devalued or to have lost momentum.

Let us pity those poor souls who in the absence of friends, family or Samaritans have to bear their sufferings alone, and whose silent screams are imploding, unheard.

I remember times when I found myself on those arctic wastes where every scream freezes the moment it has slipped over the lips - days when every morning seemed to dawn over a battlefield of body and soul, and the sun forever to hide behind a wall of clouds. Then, as on subsequent occasions, my soul was crying out like Munch's pathetic figure which, as the embodiment of loneliness and despair, has become a classic literary reference. Eventually, I would tap my inner resources; I would remember the formula which advocates self-help, patience and the counting of graces, thus restoring equilibrium.

It is said that God's mills are grinding slowly. I admit that I sometimes wish they were grinding faster or that miraculous cures were at hand. I also wish that I could summon help at the flick of a finger, whenever my soul is tempted to utter that silent scream which in Munch's unsettling picture contorts the subject's face against a background of black and white-striped isolation.

How tormented, how lonesome the artist must have been to epitomise his emotions in the form of a spine-chilling, face-warping scream.

2007

Edvard Munch: *The cry*, 1895. Lithograph.

THE FIDDLER

I met him a few years ago while I was cruising through the Mediterranean. He was the ship's star of the evening, providing musical entertainment on his fiddle. At the time he was hailed as having started a violin revolution by introducing a new style of music and catering for all moods and musical tastes. He played his instrument either with a breathtaking, Paganini-style exuberance or with the sweet whispering of a lover - a repertoire which could not fail to enthral an audience.

Being neither a Yehudi Menuhin of the classical music scene, nor a violinist leading a Palm Court orchestra, he was rated as having successfully bridged the gap between classical and popular music. He became first known in TV variety shows as the 'Sensational Violinist'. Perhaps his formula for success lay in his skill to ply the strings in turn like an Irish fiddler, a gypsy, a Latin serenader and an offbeat concert artist.

Gary Lovini may not have been a Roland Lacatos, the gypsy whom many consider to be the most accomplished violinist in the world, but to lovers of the improvisatory style and inherent romantic vein of his music - be it Bach, jazz or gypsy tunes - Lovini came allegedly a close second.

At the time a regular performer on the QEII and other cruise ships, he staged one of his shows on the SAGA Rose, the 25,000 ft cruise ship which catered exclusively for the over-fifties, among them a fair spread of septuagenarians and a handful of couples celebrating a special birthday or a wedding anniversary.

Like my fellow passengers, I was spellbound by the artist's performance, and by a programme which included popular Irish and Scottish tunes, American folk and Italian Baroque music, a full-blooded Czardas, the song 'Let it Be', and many favourites which are at home in Memory Lane.

In unison with the audience I clapped my hands; I tapped my feet to compelling rhythms or swooned to tunes to which my younger self had once been dancing, flirting or spinning amorous thoughts. As nostalgia swept through the ship's ballroom, I travelled back to the Forties and Fifties, remembering, smiling. I was young again. I was pretty, I was in love...

Judging by the rapt faces of my fellow passengers, it was clear that I was not the only one recalling memory's green pastures, not the only one to feel colour rising in her cheeks. The handsome Merlin of the violin had cast a spell on us. In my mind I saw the oldie brigade rising from their seats, their bodies swinging to the music and barely restraining themselves from dancing on the spot.

I had a vision of the Pied Piper of Hamelin; of the rats and children who could not resist the lure of his piped tunes. 'And step by step they came dancing', wrote Robert Browning in his poem The Pied Piper of Hamelin. What if the magician were to lead the way with his violin, I wondered. Would we follow the fiddler?

Final applause broke the spell and terminated my excursion into the world of fancy.

The artist gave an encore. He played 'Land of Hope and Glory'. And now the audience became very British and nostalgically, patriotic. As they lustily formed a chorus, the ballroom turned into the Albert Hall, the event into the Last Night of the Proms.

The magic had snapped. But I was still smiling.

2005

BEASTS AND BEASTIES

I have never had to live with the fear of scorpions and other venomous arachnids, nor did lions and tigers ever consider me a tasty meal. Equally, I was never in danger of being bitten by any number of disease-carrying or flesh-eating bugs, nor threatened by poisonous snakes, while the nearest I ever came to a boa constrictor was in an aquarium.

When bathing in rivers or in the sea, I did not have to be afraid of sharks, crocodiles or an onslaught of piranhas, nor of the stealthy, fatal body invasion of parasitic worms. And not even in nightmarish dreams was I ever caught unawares by a stampede of elephants or wildebeests, nor did I arouse the aggressiveness of South American killer bees. In all, although I have travelled widely on the Continent and further afield, I think I am fortunate in that I mainly had to cope with lesser, harmless beasties, such as house flies, spiders, mice, mosquitoes and wasps, not forgetting seasonal garden pests, thieving squirrels, nest-robbing magpies and bird-hunting felines, all of which are mere inconveniences when compared with flying, water-infesting, predatory and other life- or health-threatening species of the tropical and sub-tropical animal kingdom.

Yet while living in Hong Kong with my family in the Sixties, I reluctantly had to share the habitat of snakes, monkeys, wild dogs, rats, microscopic endemic bugs and other native beasties. Apart from specific viruses that were known to cause 'Hong Kong flu', 'Hong Kong tummy' and 'Hong Kong ear', more serious bacterial diseases, such as cholera, would at times enter the Colony via the hundreds of refugees who flocked into its safe haven every day. British ex-patriates were regularly vaccinated against the disease, while in food preparation special precautions were advocated against water-borne infections. There was, however, no way one could avoid occasional contact with larger beasties, whether of the spine-chilling or potentially dangerous kind.

For me, topping the list of fearsome Hong Kong vermin were the two species of common cockroach or *Blatta orientalis*. The colour of polished mahogany, these orthopterous insects were omnivorous and mostly nocturnal raiders. Kitchen cockroaches did not hunt alone, but made their forays in scurrying, strategically-operating armies. They would squeeze through the narrowest of spaces, and their sense of smell would locate every crumb of bread, every iota of food not hermetically sealed away. To see such an armoured brigade foraging in the kitchen at nightfall, examining the floor, work surfaces and draining board, was the stuff of which nightmares are made. They also seemed to have a cat's nine lives, for their shell-like armour did not squash easily underfoot, and trying to kill any such repulsive customer outright would involve the reluctant host in a battle of wits and several murderous strikes.

I still remember with a shudder the kitchen cockroach's notorious cousin which was twice its size. A miniature *pterodactyl* or giant winged beetle, this species had a habit of entering through open windows at night, seeking out whatever was its preference, which seemed to include human blood and its serum. If windows were shut, these monsters would crash against the panes with a metallic thud, before looking for access elsewhere.

Once two giant winged cockroaches nearly caused me a heart attack. During a particularly oppressive summer night, I had left the windows wide open and the curtains undrawn, in order to allow cooler night air to assist in sleep. I was brutally awoken around midnight by a sharp pain in my finger. There, on my pillow, inches away from my face and brilliantly illuminated by moonlight, were two specimens feasting on an open cut. Needless to say, in this spectral setting my heart was thumping away as after a competitive hundred-metre sprint. My shriek woke my husband, who was not amused at being

77

roused from sleep, and it was left to me to take retaliatory action against these two bloodthirsty attackers. However, possibly used to persecution by humans, they managed to evade my slipper and flew back out of the window. Still shaking, I thoroughly washed and disinfected my finger, before hiding the cut under a plaster. Then I drew the curtains and sweated out the rest of the night in uneasy dreams.

The Colony was also populated by Chinese cobras, rattlesnakes and adders, some of which sometimes found their way into homes. And as if such potential encroachment were not enough, the presence of ants or other exotic creepy-crawlies on the march in army strength for a free meal, might call for the human eradicator. Moreover, hordes of sickly-looking stray dogs and cats would stalk the scraps haven of city markets and raid domestic rubbish bins. As these canine and feline outcasts represented an all too real danger of rabies, any sensible person would abstain from getting too close to, or trying to stroke such animals. Yet while strolling one day through Kowloon City market with my children, son Number Two - as the Chinese like to list their offspring - tried to pat a mongrel while my attention momentarily dwelt on some revolting, unidentifiable food item. The animal, probably used more to kicks than to affectionate gestures, bit the child, snarled and bared its teeth until we were out of sight. As there had been a recent incident of rabies, I thought it wise to seek immediate medical attention. As a result, the doctor alerted the police, who mounted a major operation to find the bite-happy beast. Incredibly, when found, the dog was still sitting under the same market stall, snarling and baring its teeth to the dog handler in undisguised hostility. It was caught and tested negative for rabies, so our worst fears, heaven be thanked, did not materialise.

While a Hong Kong housewife might now and again be scared out of her wits by a snake lying curled up in her living-room or kitchen, there was always a risk of treading on an adder or other venomous serpent in the jungle-like territory behind the high-rise housing estate of Kowloon. Walkers were advised to be watchful of snakes lurking in the saw-edged grass, among clumps of bamboo, along dried-up water channels and, above all, in the dense tangle of undergrowth, in which tigers and other cats were occasionally spotted.

Snakes also favoured the ambience of golf courses. One day, my husband neatly hooked a three-foot viper out of the rough in which, seconds earlier, I had been searching for a stray ball. On another occasion, he would not hole the ball for a par, because a snake with ominous zigzag marks lay curled up around the flagpole, ready to spit venom at the putter which would try to shift it. Not inclined to perform any heroics, my husband sensibly abstained from moving the obstacle and accorded himself a par on his score card.

Walkers in the New Territories not familiar with jealousy in the simian kingdom, might also be taught a painful lesson. Often enough we encountered pink-faced monkeys swinging through the trees or barring our track in the manner of Third World beggar children. What we did not know was that apart from pestering rural food vendors, males could also be aggressive when roused by jealousy.

Once, during a Sunday stroll along a well-trodden path through jungle-like vegetation, a female monkey stopped us in our tracks. She was sitting at the edge of the path in the manner of a human roadside beggar, her head slightly tilted, a hand outstretched in silent appeal. My husband, fascinated by such a cute, mock-human display of begging, offered her a piece of banana. Suddenly, a jealous male monkey catapulted out of the trees and bit his apparent rival in the leg. It was a nasty bite which needed immediate medical attention. For days my husband limped around with a dour face, cursing his simian assailant. Needless to say, he never fed a wild monkey again, whatever its sex.

Rats, as it is well-known, abandon sewers during floods. They less frequently find themselves trapped in toilet basins. But that was exactly what happened one night in our Kowloon flat, an experience which left the adults cringing with disgust, while our five year-old son was greatly excited at having encountered a rat in such an unlikely location. 'Mummy', he cried, prodding me awake at an early hour, 'there's 'Ratty' in the lavatory.' On examination I found a large specimen trying to clamber out of the bowl. Male assistance had to be called for, and eventually my husband managed to flush the intruder back into the sewer.

Next morning I gave my little rat-spotter a lecture on vermin. Trying not to destroy the toddler's picture-book image of 'Ratty', I explained that the hopeful invader was an evil disease-carrying cousin of 'Ratty', which must at all costs be kept away from homes and surroundings.

'Has Mole also got an evil cousin?' asked the keen reader of the children's classic. I replied in the negative, not wishing to elaborate on those small mammals which are the curse of gardeners who like their lawn to be as smooth as a golfing green. And while we were hot on the subject, I gathered the children around me and told them about man's uneasy relationship with beasts and beasties, and the loveable role some animals play in children's story and picture-books.

All this happened many years ago, and who knows what modern methods have since been employed to clear urban areas of cockroaches, and other vermin, and whether the continuing replacement of Kowloon's subtropical hinterland with new housing estates has driven snakes and big cats further inland.

I now live in a quiet rural corner of East Kent, where thanks to Rentokil, farm pesticides, domestic traps and specific poisons, verminous creatures are less evident, and where predatory beasts, monkeys and large snakes live behind bars in zoos. Well, some at least most of the time. For occasionally, animals normally associated with the jungle or African plains do escape from their cages or seek a new habitat. Apart from an increasing number of foxes, feral cats are now regularly reported to kill farmyard fowl and lambs, while a panther-like creature is being frequently sighted in the Scottish Highlands. Adders have also moved closer to human habitations. While Londoners have to watch out for suspicious-looking, lethal packages planted by ruthless and dastardly man-beasts, English country-dwellers have been told to be wary of adders and their poisonous sting. Driven out of their natural habitat by farmers and developers, they are now increasingly spotted in people's gardens.

And what about the vulture who, having escaped from captivity for a lofty bird's eye view and an avian giggle, recently enjoyed a week of freedom? Sweeping regally over the roofs of houses, or sitting in the crown of trees, I am sure the bird was highly amused at the public interest it caused, and was it my imagination or did it cock a beaky snook at his hopeful captors below?

Indeed, beasts and beasties are getting smarter all the time. What about the chimp, I ask, which not long ago picked the mobile phone from his keeper's pocket and over three nights plagued zoo staff with anonymous calls, breathing heavily?

What next? I wonder. Will the time come when shoppers in the High Street are stopped by a gorilla beating its chest, encounter a crocodile or shark in the waters off Bexhill-on-Sea, or find a tarantula or other loathsome beastie nibbling away in our cartons of cornflakes?

Not wishing to interfere with Nature, I have to tolerate nest-robbing magpies, food-thieving squirrels and the odd pheasant or moorhen stalking through my flower beds oblivious to the tender blooms of annuals. And I can only growl and bark like a Rottweiler at prowling cats on the lookout for birds. But then I take up seasonal arms against slugs and snails, wasps, kitchen flies, vine weevils and greenfly, and come winter, against mice seeking warm quarters in my house as non-paying lodgers and food seekers. It is, after all MY house, I maintain, and I have paid off my mortgage. It is also MY garden, cultivated and seasonally tended with great back-breaking effort and costs. So why should it be Arcadia for common garden pests?

And now it is time again to inspect my roses for black spot and my lupins for slug damage. With my swatter at hand, I am also ready to deliver any sting-happy or irksome insect to netherland.

2006

THE KILLING FIELDS

Last night I went out in the garden to find out which creatures so shamelessly serrated the tender leaves of plants and so often reduced them to bare stalks. As under a new spring moon the garden was steeped in darkness, a weird spectacle met the beam of my torch: no gambolling young foxes, no hares nosing each other in a foreplay to mating. Nor was it my old friend Arthur, the badger, who often strode across the lawn around midnight as if on a catwalk. No, out in corporate strength an army of slugs and snails had gathered on grass, around flower tubs and on the patio. More were approaching from all directions, antennae wiggling. Some were slugging along in a marching column, others were first making a meal of some foliage before joining what looked like a copulating ritual. Cringing in disgust, I surveyed the molluscan Glastonbury, then fetched some slug pellets. I had not taken recourse to such a drastic killing method before, as a beer-filled trap had allowed one or the other to binge drink and die happily. Yet, I felt merciless on this occasion. Having liberally sprinkled the poison around them, the scene was set to turn into killing fields. Somehow I felt very mean and close to apologising to the doomed pests, and I went back to bed troubled by a whiff of nausea, just as if I had flicked a huge black spider off my bedclothes. Just as in Hong Kong one steaming night, when I woke to two enormous winged cockroaches taking a bite out of a badly healed wound on my finger.

I got up early next morning, feeling uneasy about my nocturnal ambush. I also realised that dead slugs and snails would be lying around in a yellow, blue-tinted gelatinous mess, and I thus lost no time in clearing the killing fields. As I shovelled and disposed of the carcasses, revulsion kept any thought of breakfast at bay.

A few days later, in a bizarre turn of events, I found a king-sized snail firmly enthroned on the roof of my garaged

Polo. Had the mollusc ventured up there via a tyre and the car's innards because it fancied a ride? And as if this phenomenon were not enough, I discovered an outsized slug nibbling happily away at a juicy begonia leaf in my veranda hanging basket - a climb surely equalling Edmund Hillary's feat on Everest. Now, were these two members of the hated species making a statement that as a pest slugs and snails were here to stay whatever gardeners' murderous strikes? Or were the two survivors exacting revenge on me? Grinding my teeth, I sent them to an early grave.

This year, I am happy to report that the number of gastropods has spectacularly decreased. This may be due in part to a larger trap filled with expensive export brew, and to the work of my feathered friends who - well-fed in the worm and berry-less season - seek out unwanted visitors for a gourmet protein-enriched meal. It certainly makes for a happy gardener. For with slug pellets banned from my eco-garden, I now find only empty shells and the odd slimy trace, while - with ravage-free foliage - blooms normally favoured by molluscan invaders now have a chance to become prize exhibits at the annual village flower show.

2001

PET HATES

Hatred is a powerful negative emotion. Like fear, jealousy and other similarly festering sentiments, it will gradually erode the soul, if not the very substance of one's life. I feel that I am fortunate in that I am incapable of hating anything or anybody in the real sense of the word. We may frequently say 'I hate' this and that, and we may have strong feelings about the way some people behave or broadcast their attitudes, but these won't cause us sleepless nights nor grow dominant. They are merely 'pet hates' without the animus or passion that 'hatred' implies.

Jenny Joseph says in her acclaimed poem 'Warning', in which she lists the eccentricities in which old people may indulge with impunity: 'When I am an old woman, I shall wear purple/With a red hat which doesn't go, and which doesn't suit me.' Apart from other examples of whimsical behaviour, such as wearing terrible shirts, spitting in public, sitting down on the pavement for a rest and pressing alarm bells, she anticipates the freedom of running her stick along public railings and picking flowers from other people's gardens. Old age, she intimates, is a free ticket to indulgences which in one's youth or middle age are frowned upon, and with which one may make up for the sobriety of one's youth.

Now this is where, in its mildest form, my pet hates come in. I, for one, shall not wear purple, a colour which, like black, and for no apparent reason, I 'hate'. Neither shall I wear a red hat, which in my dress vocabulary is the prerogative of young, smart women. I shall not wear shirts that make people frown or giggle, and I shall definitely steer clear of alarm bells and restrain myself from picking other people's flowers, something I don't see as a caprice of old age, but as an unwritten taboo. (However, who will not admit to having picked the odd flower from across some fence when nobody was looking?)

Needless to say, I 'hate' people spitting in public, particularly the gusty expectorations of bronchitic old dears. I also shall not sit down on the pavement for a rest, as this might not so much point to odd behaviour in one so obviously mature, but to homelessness or an act of advanced senility (all the more if I were dressed in purple and wore a red hat).

No, I shall not wear purple with a red hat, nor do any of the things that Jenny Joseph warns the readers she will do when she is old. I believe old people do not hold a franchise to behave in ways traditionally considered anti-social, shocking or unbecoming. I love Jenny Joseph's poem, though. And I don't know what my walking stick might do, when I pass a public railing.

What old age entitles one to do in my book is openly to air one's views and be frank about one's pet hates. Nobody will take notice of them anyway, and if they do, they will blame the generation gap or a weird gene.

Pet hates are always of a personal nature. They don't imply the powerful emotion of 'hatred', but are harmless, often critical statements that, apart from pointing to age-related attitudes, may indicate idiosyncrasies, changes in society or education-bred sensitivities. Frequently they are no more than humorous observations in a minor key. They will achieve nothing, and they are seldom being aired on a public platform. Pet hates may embrace a host of sentiments ranging from mere dislikes in their gentlest form to more potent distastes.

I am but one of many who reserve a special pet hate for those who happily ravish the English language by substituting every second adjective with a four-letter word. I feel hostile towards tea-ladies at station buffets or in cafeterias who, while chatting away, are whirling a tea-bag around in a mug for less than five seconds, before presenting the brew as 'tea'.

When playing bridge, I feel my patience being sorely tried by the player who in working out a bid, or which card to lead or discard, takes so long over it that other players may easily forget which suit is trumps or how many cards of a particular suit have been played, something on which a good player likes to focus his concentration. On the other hand, when playing Scrabble, I could happily shoot the opposition who, while ruminating and cogitating about how to achieve a seven-letter word, or how to make the most of triple and double counts, make me doze off or plan a journey to the Antipodes. I find wobbly tables irritating, on which hot liquids crash over the rim of cups like breakers; I develop an instant antipathy towards strangers who, thirty seconds into a conversation, ask me 'Where do you come from?' I disdain the sight of well-dressed, respectable burghers drinking beer from the bottle, and I could cheerfully strangle neighbours whose thunderous petrol-driven lawnmowers, electric hedge cutters or drills will go into action on hot summer afternoons when, with my body hugging a comfy garden chair, my mind is eulogising about the beautiful peace and quiet of my rural abode. (In Germany, where enforced rules have governed citizens' lives since the Kaiser's era, the time for mowing lawns, beating carpets and engaging in any noisy DIY activities is restricted to a few hours in the mornings and afternoons on weekdays, setting aside the hours between one and three in the afternoon for Mittagsschlaf, the siesta period which used to be a national middle-class institution.)

As one who ranks politeness and good manners as essential virtues, I feel strongly about people whose tight lips and inhospitable demeanour do not allow them to say 'Please' and 'Thank you', or whose eating habits resemble those of Cro-Magnon Man.

One pet hate of mine is loquacity. Seemingly for hours, some people will be chatting away like talking robots, leaving no room for one to interject or present one's views. Satisfied

87

with the listener's occasional nod of agreement, a raise of eyebrows or whatever facial contortions will denote amazement, approval or incredulity, they lose their sense of time, and only by brutally cleaving into the barrage of words may one get oneself heard.

Although I am reasonably tolerant of the antics and fashion trends of the younger generation, I realise that many adolescents like to shock their elders with an unconventional, if not freakish appearance with which they are aping their peers or trying to express their personality. However, I cannot abide the lack of good manners and selfish behaviour one so frequently witnesses in young adults nowadays. I deplore the ignorance, or outright defiance by the hard core, of what is right and wrong, that is, what the Bible, the Law and common decency define as 'right'. As a Christian my voice is swallowed by the dialectics of those who declare the Ten Commandments and Articles of Faith to be mumbo-jumbo, and who, swept along by the moral effluent of society, subscribe to a philosophy which allows them to make up their own rules of self-indulgence, no matter how many victims or moral standards are falling by the wayside.

I don't understand why some black-clad, black-haired girls paint their lips a mauvish-black and make their eyes look like black pools of sin. Do they fancy themselves as satanic priestesses? I don't understand why, like medieval circus freaks, some young adults spike their hair and dye it a garish colour, or why so many in tribal fashion have parts of their bodies gold-ringed or studded. Are they so desperate to stand out in the crowd, so anxious to shock, non-conform or express their individuality? I shake my head in disbelief at adolescents and adult males who have their bodies extensively tattooed with erotic or macho symbols, and I shall forever fail to see why many men are wearing what, for me, are effeminate earrings, or why in increasing numbers they shave their heads, when nature has endowed them with a fine crop of hair. But then, as history shows, there is no limit to the dictates of fashion and its unconventional or weird side-shows. Thus tolerance would seem to be called for.

I will admit, though, to 'hating' the practices of pre-pubescent males and young men who on quiet country estates or urban terraces will have their transistor radios blasting and thumping away with metal music. Or who will rev the engines of their mopeds and motorcycles to imitate the din of the Isle of Man track, just to annoy residents.

I reserve a special pet hate for those youngsters and able-bodied citizens who will not give up their seat on a crowded bus or train to a heavily pregnant woman or an elderly person. But then good manners and consideration for others start in the nursery, and such education is sadly lacking in many families today.

Admittedly, these are all minor, hardly arguable hates of mine, most of which I attribute to my advanced years and to changes in our society, if not to a nostalgia by my generation for the moral values, codes of behaviour and national pride which provided the nation's backbone during the war and the spartan post-war years.

I find it hard, however, not to hate paedophiles and child abusers, as well as all those who can kill a human being as they would swat a fly. I despise football hooligans and the army of thugs who live for nothing but violence and the excitement of causing damage and destruction. In this I join those law-abiding citizens who anxiously witness young people drifting into a lawless hinterland, soon to join a callous, crime-, drink- and drug-related underclass which is spreading its sub-culture through society like a cancer. In their often appalling, unblinkingly committed crimes I truly see the Antichrist at work.

Yet when I read about juvenile delinquents, particularly the under-tens, I tend to look for psychologically mitigating circumstances, mindless or mind-boggling as the children's crimes may be, and as little respect as they may show for a person's life or property. I may feel angry at the insolence and destructive behaviour of the streetwise; I may, as in the James Bulger case, see young minds perverted by evil, where childhood innocence should still prevail or some inborn barrier prevent children committing hideous acts. Rather than hate these young criminals, whom one outraged citizen once called 'the devil's apprentices', I pity them. For many do not know any better. Many never had a chance to learn the ABC of Right and Wrong. They are, after all, the product of our society, in which all sexual taboos have fallen and manic shopping, corruption, the hunt for status symbols and the accumulation of riches have dropped moral values and charity from many adults' vocabulary.

One of my pet hates erupted in the early Eighties, when there was a sharp rise in Salmonella and other bacterial food poisoning from the handling of raw minced beef and cooked meats.

I was living in Glasgow at the time, and when shopping I often watched with disbelief, if not feelings of disgust, how assistants in butcher's shops and at supermarket meat counters were slicing, stacking and prettily arranging cooked ham, or scooping minced beef, with their bare hands. In many butcher's shops I was horrified to see blood-reddened fingers handling money after each purchase. All too often, mince was being kneaded and shaped like artist's clay. Worse still, female assistants might interrupt their slicing and fondling of cooked ham and sausage, by putting away a stray lock of hair or indulging in some other unhygienic habit likely to contaminate the goods they were serving.

In those days the bug-counting shopper and poet in me wrote the following poem which appeared in the local paper:

NEXT, PLEASE

Like half-closed curtains
greasy hair is straggling
down her face that holds
but youth, bland unconcern
and angry pimples,
and in her eyes both night
and morning meet.

Her long-nailed hand
in weary gesture
pushes back a lock
that hampered vision,
then fingers, absent-minded,
an earringed lobe.

Now plunges lustily,
its grab wide open,
into the blood-red fibrous mass,
extracting a full load,
now dropping ounce by ounce
onto the scale,
forming a pyramid.

Skilfully, the hand now shapes
the patient mixture,
is squaring, rounding, patting.
A sculptress at work?
A child at play?
Indeed, was that a smile?

Now, to complete the cycle,
one pound of lean minced beef
is changing hands;
fingers, still damp and pink,
receive reluctant notes,
count up the change.

Next, please!

I like to think that the poem inspired local Department of Health inspectors to make the use of gloves and tongs mandatory in butchers' shops and at supermarket meat counters.

2002

PICTURES AT AN EXHIBITION

In May 2001, I visited the Special Exhibition 'Spirit of the Ages' at the National Gallery, London. It proved to be another 'special' experience for me.

This time many exhibits created déjà vu sentiments. Memories drew me into scenes, set-pieces and half-forgotten landscapes. On loan from Berlin's National Gallery were paintings by German nineteenth century Romantic artists, among them a range from the former East German Republic, which following Germany's Reunification had found a new home in the National Gallery of the new capital.

I once described my mind's ability to step into a picture which strikes a certain chord in me. During such momentary emotional transport my perception of sounds and movements around me seems to dull, thus creating a near perfect ambience for recall and aiding that special, if fleeting, experience. Here, moreover, I was confronted not only with a period with which I was familiar through the study of history, but also with paintings of landscapes and figures which during my life in Germany I had come to know and love. Such pre-knowledge now qualified me as a visitor, not as an intruder from another age.

The Exhibition included paintings by artists who are household names in Germany, but of which the British art-loving public is widely ignorant, primarily because it seldom has a chance to view such an eclectic show.

Paintings by Friedrich Schinkel, the architect who transformed Berlin with his monumental buildings, depicted aspects of the Kaiser and my grandparents' Berlin. They complemented the much-loved works of Caspar David Friedrich and Adolph Menzel, the artists who had always occupied a special place in my appreciation of German Romanticism. Lesser known masterpieces by Moritz Schwind, Karl Blechen, Max Liebermann, Hans Thomas, Max

Beckmann and Covis Corinth provided fascinating viewing and further evoked interest in the German Romantic art movement.

As I walked through the Gallery, my memories worked overtime. Caspar David Friedrich's depiction of Solitary Oak Tree In The Snow brought back images of bomb-torn Berlin early in 1945. For a heart-rending flash of time, I was back to the morning which, while still holding the terror of the night, had filled me with a deep sense of gratitude for having survived once again.

The building opposite had been reduced to a skeletal façade and rubble by an Allied aerial mine. Our house, and the lives of its occupants, had been spared.

I vividly remember that morning. I was looking out of what was left of our front windows, giant holes bereft of glass and frames. A red sun was rising over a snow-blanketed urban scene, and behind an oak tree whose top had been blown off by the blast of the bomb. Its scarred branches were reaching out to the sky in a helpless gesture or, seen against the adjacent destruction, as a monument to life's transience. Just as Friedrich's Solitary Oak Tree.

Friedrich's painting Das Riesengebirge shows a man looking across the range of what pre-war used to be part-Silesian, part Bohemian mountains. At the feet of the only figure there featured Der Teich, a large mountain lake. This painting transported me back to the summer holiday, when my father and I had walked through those hills. I remember trekking uphill through dense pine forests, along gurgling brooks and carpets of blueberries. Tired and happy, we had sat down at the edge of the Teich, just like Friedrich's lonely figure, and unpacked our picnic fare. We admired the view across the lake and towards the distant rounded peaks, the same view which - according to the history of the picture - the artist had sketched on his walking holiday through the Riesengebirge: the seemingly infinite hilltops which in the painting melt with a luminous horizon, a sight which Friedrich is said to have interpreted as holding the promise of

93

Redemption. Nothing of this had entered the mind of the fourteen year-old girl at the time. I was enjoying my cheese rolls and black bread lard sandwiches, while looking forward to a visit of the Spindler-Baude[1] on our way down, where there would be Silesian Streusselkuchen and a man playing the zither. Now and then I would look around me, half expecting Rübezahl, the mystical, gentle giant, to appear from behind some boulder.

On my way through the Gallery I came across a painting which for me was perhaps the highlight of the exhibition. Beautifully gilt-framed, as befitted Adolph Menzel's famous picture, and dominating the entire wall of one room, was Frederick the Great's Flute Concert In The Palace Of Sanssouci. In the concert hall of the Schloss, under sparkling chandeliers, and surrounded by elegantly-attired courtiers, the king was playing one of his own compositions for the flute, accompanied by a chamber ensemble which included Emmanuel Bach and other notable musicians of the time. The exquisite harmony of golden colours and shimmering candle-light, as well as the sumptuousness of the ladies' crinoline dresses, make the picture a veritable feast for the eye. For me, though, it was more. It dug up immediate images of my grandmother's drawing room in Berlin before the war: of an expensively gilt-framed, if smaller-sized, copy of the Flute Concert hanging over the shiny grand piano and lending infinite elegance to the room; of a time, ultimately, when I was still blind to the aesthetics of Art and Beauty, and its cultivation.

Menzel's painting Supper At The Ball is also a study of minute detail. Crowding a palatial ballroom, members of Berlin's late nineteenth century society are talking animatedly, while balancing their supper plates. Many of the men are in gala uniform, with decorations pinned to their chests. The ladies are delicately coiffured and in low décolleté dresses, their satin and lace and jewellery adding a luxury note to the

---

[1] A timbered mountain café and restaurant

sheen of graduated candlelight. The picture represents a perfect composition of German upper bourgeoisie and military society at the turn of the century, my grandmother's time, and one of the gala events she and my grandfather may have attended.

Caspar David Friedrich's Solitary Oak Tree stands in a bleak expanse, naked, its storm-scarred branches reaching towards heaven as in silent despair. For me the tree's solitariness symbolised loneliness. While the artist's interpretation had been a philosophical one - the life force of Nature, and the intermediacy between Earth and Heaven - the picture poignantly mirrored moments in my life, when I had been languishing in the same mood which the tree and its ambience imparted.

Adolph Menzel's The Potsdam-Berlin Railway also made me take a time leap. The painting depicts the first steam train plying between the Prussian city and the capital. What looks like an adult version of Thomas the Tank Engine is tugging toy-sized wagons through a flat rural landscape that is not yet marred by housing developments, motorways and pylons. In the distance, the hazy outlines of roofs, a church steeple and the cupola of the Potsdam dome. This picture also found a resonance in me. For, in the early Thirties, a more powerful engine used to pull a 20th century variant of the train. I remember it chuffing past my grandmother's house. Now at an hourly service, it was running through mainly built-up areas and the mature pine forests of the Mark Brandenburg. I remember many rides on the train, accompanying my mother or grandmother on a shopping spree into the city.

One morning during a school holiday spent at my grandmother's house, I was told we were about to take the last ride on the train. There were garlands, flowers and even wreaths at every station. The single, wooden-seat compartments were packed with travellers savouring what in engineering terms spelt the dawn of an electrically-driven suburban railway era. Shortly afterwards, the S-Bahn came to replace what Menzel had once painted as the first German city shuttle-train of the industrial age. And it was not long before my grandmother and I tried out this new steamless means of communication. We were both excited and, like other passengers, a little fearful of the automatic doors. We marvelled at the latest feat of German railway engineering and, having got off at our destination, felt we were now part of some local historical event.

From that day I came to use the S-Bahn frequently. It survived the war, and when Berlin was sectioned off, it came under the jurisdiction of the East German Communist government, which allowed it to age disgracefully. Furthermore, with its terminals in the Eastern Sector, Stasi[1] spies were known conveniently to filter into Western Sectors. Allegedly there had been occasions when politically vulnerable persons on the train, identified by Stasi personnel, became easy prey. Running the train through the Western Sectors without stopping, such persons would be arrested at Friedrichstrasse, the first station in the Eastern Sector. For the possibility of such scenarios alone, the S-Bahn during the Cold War was an unloved and, for many people, a fear-inspiring means of transport.

Following German Reunification, the Bonn Government and the Berlin Senate gave the S-Bahn a much-needed facelift, repaired the track and extended its network to outlying districts. All that is left now of the early Potsdam-Berlin steam train are artists' impressions and early sepia photographs.

There were other paintings which impelled me to stand and stare and enjoy the messages of an era in which Romanticism found its expression in Art and Literature; a period, ultimately, which despite the non-culture of twentieth century society, never ceases to excite and, here and there, evokes sentiments of nostalgia.

2002

---

[1] East German Secret Police

CHASING THE WIND

Methuselah is said to have lived to a mind-boggling 969 years. Yet the Hebrew Bible does not tell us whether he achieved such longevity by the grace of God or due to a genetic oversight. To me, to live so long would amount to centuries of living hell. As I have passed the age which Shakespeare so delicately phrased as one 'without teeth, without hair, without eyes, without anything', the very thought of finally slipping into mental and physical decrepitude does not make for happy moments. Now and then I may inwardly groan at the various afflictions of old age; I may be uncomfortably aware of the 'dying of the light' which Dylan Thomas urges us to 'fight, fight, against'; I may be saddened by my ever-narrowing physical boundaries; I may hear the clock ticking ever faster and more noisily. Yet despite many handicaps I am content. Content with what I have and what I have achieved. And at last I know that all that there was had to be. I realise that my convoluted course of life, all my physical and mental suffering, as well as many new beginnings, had a purpose: the aim to make me what I am today.

'Life is useless', proclaims the Philosopher in the *Ecclesiastes*, as he muses over the shortness of human life, its injustices and frustrations. 'It is like chasing the wind', he says, because people are never satisfied with what they have. Yet such discontent only lends weight to the argument that if early man had been content with his lot, his mental powers and physical potential, and if, furthermore, he had never tried to explore the world beyond his visible horizon, humankind would surely have stopped at the evolutionary stage of early cave-dwellers.

Perhaps true contentment with what one has achieved within one's mental, physical and educational confines does not come until one has reached a certain age - an age of acceptance that requires a grain of wisdom, as does the final realisation that whatever there was, had to be.

But then not everyone is blessed with such insight. Provided we suffer no basic needs or have to live with constant pain, grief, guilt or loneliness, contentment will come with inner peace and zephyr-like moments of happiness. Still, we may ask ourselves sometimes where all the songs of spring have gone, or we may be aching for what in all its splendour now only vibrates in the memory.

Thankfully, advanced age in our climate of ageism comes with a certain *carte blanche*, a freedom which allows us - at least occasionally - to behave like children or eccentrics. Instead of knitting, playing bingo, watching mindless TV programmes or conforming to the traditional image of 'old dears', we ladies may wear an Ascot hat to where jeans and T-shirts are *de rigeur*; we may paint our fingernails green or crimson, or apply for the part of the witch in the local amateur production of Hänsel and Gretel. Men might sport pink ties, or wear Nike trainers with a George Melly suit and don a baseball cap back to front. No limits are set for a great break-out from an age-dictated regime. And what about a ride in a balloon, taking part in a rally, learning to abseil or opting for some other daredevil pursuit that will have the hair of neighbours and loved ones standing up, and make them question whether we are still of sound mind? Travel, too, will sweeten old age. If health and finance allow, why not holiday in some Shangri-La to which the inner eye has always strayed? Why not venture to the wadis of the Sahara, the remains of Xanadu, the lonely Ayers Rock or the treasures of Istanbul? Why, indeed, not have a last fling before life puts on the brakes?

Some of us 'oldies' may find strength in what there remains, by trying to drain the last drop of Omar Khayyám's cup of earthly delights; others might find it difficult to come to terms with ageing and old age, intent on setting the clock back by means of costly products and treatments hailed by the anti-wrinkle industry for their rejuvenating effect. Dreading the sound of the Last Post, and what there may lie behind - if anything - they continue to chase the wind.

Sadly, it will take most of us half a lifetime before we will accept what can no longer be; before we can say, 'I am content with what I am and what I have.' Before, ultimately, we reach the conclusion that whatever there has been in our life, whether good or bad, had to be, in order to make us what we are today.

And since we are no longer chasing the wind, we may now fight against the 'dying of the light', by trying to live every day to the full, always on the lookout for what elevates us spiritually and makes living still a worthwhile task.

2005

I MUST GO DOWN TO THE SEA AGAIN

For the best of my life I was a landlubber. I grew up in level urban landscapes, in which a man-made rubble mountain or a slag heap would have stuck out like Ayers Rock. For many years I set foot in the mountains only during walking or skiing holidays. Yet it was on such occasions that I came to love the challenge of heights. In later years I was never happier than when I had a range of hills or mountains in view. They symbolised the ups and downs of life for me, and with their ever-present challenge to climb them, they somehow willed me to manage every steep ascent I was facing in my affairs. I now live next to a range of gently meandering, sheep-grazed heights on which single solitary trees defy the strong winds that often sweep through this Kentish valley.

When I was a teenager I spent winter holidays skiing in the Riesengebirge, the Silesian pine-clad mountains which after the war went to Poland and Czechoslovakia. I remember crystal-clear water flowing over smooth stone, forming sleepy ponds between rocks or crashing down a hillside. I remember the well-trodden paths leading up to the *Schneekoppe*, and the pine-wooded slopes carpeted in August with fat blueberries. Part of the charm of the Riesengebirge were the cosy *Bauden*[1] which served Silesian *Streusselkuchen* to the sound of zither music. And whether rambling through the hills, standing at a glacial lake or resting by a gurgling brook, one was always aware of the presence of Rübezahl, the wise and benevolent mountain spirit who, as legend has it, would be here and there and everywhere, guiding and protecting the wanderer.

I also spent winter holidays in the Harz mountains, the Erzgebirge and the Bavarian Alps. Snow was never a problem, and temperatures often plummeted, so that skis would be gliding over the snow as over splintered glass. Ski lifts were

---

[1] Local mountain inns

still rare in those days, and skiers had to make it up to a piste or some glacial downhill run on foot, carrying skis over their shoulders. Perhaps such effort held a greater sense of achievement than being winched up in today's chair lifts and cable cars.

One pre-war Christmas Eve which, as a ten-year old I spent in the Riesengebirge with my father, stands out in my memory: like pilgrims, we were tramping through the deep snow to a tiny Norwegian timber church embedded in the mountainside. A clear moonlit night. Bells ringing for the *Weihnachts-Mette*[1] like glass chimes. Snow crunching, sighing under our boots, and above us the stars shining as brightly as I thought they must have done once over the Nativity scene.

Another cameo of memory was formed one New Year's Eve during the war in the Erzegebirge, the Saxonian and Bohemian mountain range. Celebrating *Silvester*[2] in a *Skihütte*, I was part of a group of young people, laughing, singing, drinking hot punch and dancing to the music of an accordion. At the stroke of midnight our party skied down to the valley in daring parallel turns, each of us holding a burning torch, and the young men among us - young soldiers on leave - not counting the hours or days back to the front…

Why then, if I have such potent memories of mountain holidays, and such apparent affinity with every mount, do I so love the sea? The sea is not in my blood. No ancestors have captained ships or sailed with the trade winds. Hills and mountains do attract me with their own brand of magnetism, but the wide open spaces of the sea create a mental freedom which delivers my thoughts to a high level of consciousness. I came to know the sea at its angriest and at its calmest, shimmering best. I swam in it when no nasty bugs were lurking under its surface and it carried no man-made detritus. I cruised through the Mediterranean, the Baltic Sea and the Atlantic; on

[1] Christian Midnight Service
[2] New Year's Eve

a freighter I crossed the Indian Ocean, the China Sea and the notorious waters of the Cape of Good Hope. Even storms did not tone down my love for the sea. For I found that the combination of dark, cloud-swept skies and winds whipping up the sea until it resembled a boiling cauldron held an awesome beauty. Admittedly, hurricane-like winds buffeting a ship may easily invite in some passengers a subconscious fear of their vessel capsizing and leaving survivors at the mercy of the sea. Torrential rain at sea may evoke in Bible literates visions of The Deluge; of all life on earth drowning around Noah's Ark in a flood of biblical proportions. In young minds, rough seas may conjure up images of killer sharks, giant octopuses and other sea monsters waiting to pull the ship's human cargo down to their depth.

But then, having spent themselves, the winds will change to a light breeze, the air reek of freshness and salt, and only the white spume on the appeased waters, which now no more than gently slap the hull, will remind seafarers of the elements' fickle moods.

Just as the view from the top of a mountain can be manna for the soul, so the sight of a calm sea in the full light of the sun or, especially in southern latitudes on a moonlit night, will arouse the senses and liberate the mind from things all too secular, the kind of *bella vista* which has always had a special appeal to romantic painters and to those gifted with a sense of beauty and the sublime. Indeed, who will not gasp at the sight of a night sky, in which the stars appear to be light years closer to earth? Who will not marvel at the spectacle of a full moon sending shafts of silver over the water...?

As my love for the sea grew, I came one day across the seascape pictures of the 19th century Russian painter Ivan Aivazovsky. Among the many artists who depicted the sea in its changing moods, he occupies a premier position. The average visitor to picture galleries in the West may never have heard of him, yet he is Russia's most popular romantic artist. With his paintings of swirling seas, storm-tossed vessels and grim, spray-soaked clouds, he brings the dynamic forces of the sea admirably to life. He also created many admirers with the beauty and serenity of his southern moonlit seascapes. One of them was William Turner, whose own masterpieces include the more abstract paintings *The Snowstorm* and *The Deluge*, which are rated to be the finest portrayals of cataclysmic storms at sea in all art. He once wrote a poem on the Russian's The Bay of Naples in a Moonlit Night:

> 'I see the moon all gold and silver
> Reflected in the sea below...
> And on the surface of the sea
> There plays a breeze which leaves a trail
> Of trembling ripples, like a shower
> Of fiery sparks...'

Growing up in Berlin and Potsdam, I came to know the river Havel and its lakes as a sailing, boating and bathing haven for land-locked city dwellers. Along its pine-wooded banks, outdoor cafés welcomed weekend trippers in summer with freshly-baked apple or plum cake topped with lashings of whipped cream. For one hot wartime summer, the Heiligensee in Potsdam beguiled me with its calm, sun-spun beauty, as rowing and dreaming, or swimming naked, I forgot the war and the demands of the Hitler Youth.

I first faced large stretches of water when, as a seven year-old, my parents packed me off during the school summer holidays to a children's home on the shores of the Baltic Sea, another year to one in a North Sea resort. In the former I caught chicken pox, which confined me for weeks to a sick-room whose window allowed me to see but a sliver of the amber coast. In the other, wind and rain swept the beach, and the chill waters of the North Sea did not invite young holiday-makers to swim.

A memorable encounter with the sea dates back to 1948, when as one of a group of German girls, recruited by Britain's Ministry of Labour to train as nurses or work as hospital domestics in England, I crossed the Channel in vicious November weather. I remember a veteran coaster lying restlessly at anchor in the steadily stiffening wind, and a hold which reeked of troops, tobacco and sweat. I still see before me the crested waves rolling in from a seething sea over which darkness was falling fast. It was not a passage for squeamish stomachs. 'By midnight', as I wrote in The Naked Years: 'the wind had reached gale force, and the vessel was pitching and tossing, the sea pounding against its hull as if threatening to break it apart. The moaning and retching of the bunk occupants joined the groaning and creaking of the ship. Roller-coasting, big-wheeling, riding on a merry-go-round, I felt I was serving sentence for every sin I had ever committed. With the last shred of my evening meal gone and racked with the unproductive contractions of my stomach, I no longer cared whether I reached the safety of an English harbour or ended up at the bottom of the sea.'

Thirteen years passed before I experienced a storm of that magnitude again.

My family and I were passengers on a 8,000 ton cargo boat bound for Hong Kong. Soon after we had left the Gulf of Aden and headed for the Indian Ocean, both the sky and the sea looked dark and troubled, and it was not long before a squally wind whipped up the waves and the vessel began to dance as if rudderless. By nightfall it was facing the full force of a typhoon, yielding to every gust and swell, and riding on the high waves as on a rodeo bull.

It was not the only violent storm encountered by ships on which I was a passenger. But then there were always days of clear skies, when the sea was bathed in light. In the southern hemisphere, and sometimes in more northern reaches, there were unforgettable moonlit nights in which the Milky Way resembled a wispy cloud and the ribbon of light on the water a jewelled path.

Some years ago, violent marine storms were the latest craze on the big screen. We had man-hunting sharks, dinosaurs, giant ants, venomous spiders and killer bees to attract thrill-seeking film-goers, and fans of disaster movies found themselves on the sinking Titanic. A Hollywood studio produced a film about a monster storm at sea. Based on the best-selling novel The Perfect Storm, it was hailed as an awe-inspiring blockbuster. However, its special effect 100-feet waves and some virtual reality scenes would have been unlikely entertainment for viewers prone to sea-sickness. And who knows, it may not be long before some daredevil director will make a film about The Apocalypse, the end-of-the-world as an ultimate screen shocker.

Such films are not for me. And as for marine thrills, I shall always settle for the less dramatic: a cruise or a trip to some seashore.

When I lived in Scotland I used to go down to the Ayrshire coast and walk on a deserted beach whenever I needed the view across a wide expanse of water, in order to sort out some problems in my mind. Whether the sea was calm or raked by blustering winds, whether mist veiled the Isle of Arran or the tide was out, with every footstep I left on the sand a mental puzzle would fall into place; with every wave breaking ashore in high winds, or at the sight of the changing tides, I would discard mental baggage in some cathartic process. Or I might just go down to the seaside to fill my lungs with bracing air that smelled of ocean, sea-shells and seaweed drying in the sun.

Now that I live in south-east Kent, and not far from Matthew Arnold's 'White Cliffs of England', I continue my beloved pilgrimages to the seaside in fine weather, just to look across the shimmering water and listen to the sound of the running tides and the cries of gulls. Here, riding on the waves far out to sea or rising high up into the air on the wings of a bird, I do not have to wait long before my mind ceases to be earth-bound.

Come to think of it, perhaps I did have some sea-faring ancestors who felt with John Masefield that all they needed beside the lonely sea and the sky was 'a tall ship and a star to sail her by'.

2005

ANYONE FOR BRIDGE?

Bridge, once part of English upper class culture, and in modern times the province of what is often irreverently referred to as the 'blue rinse brigade', has changed its image. No longer the privilege of retired people, bridge has become fashionable, being labelled 'hip' and sexy, a 'cool' leisure pursuit. Devotees include well-known names from the world of stage and screen, fashion houses and the arts scene. Even Bill Gates, the world's richest man, is known to have caught the bridge bug.

According to Andrew Robson, the Times' bridge columnist (who admits to being a fanatic about the card game), more and more younger players have become members of bridge clubs, because 'bored of getting drunk, they want to stretch their minds'. The Bridge Union goes further: describing itself as an up-market dating agency, they claim that bridge has a special appeal to young male city professionals who are fed up with hanging around bars or scanning the female office potential for a date. The same apparently goes for young career women who join bridge clubs for dating opportunities or in the hope of finding love. It certainly conjures up an interesting scenario. For who knows how many males may fasten their eyes on an attractive female partner or try to play footsie under the bridge table; how many young women, affected by such courting foreplay, may drop a card whilst shuffling or dealing, or suddenly find all the rules of the game going haywire in their minds?

No such undercurrents are believed to exist in clubs in which members are of post-pensionable age. In my own club, in which 'social rubber bridge' is played, the grey-haired ladies and gentlemen would look aghast at suggestions that a bridge table may be alive with erogenous vibrations. Their main object is to keep their brains from growing sluggish and senility at bay, by engaging in a mentally challenging and socially interactive pastime. Yet even in their declining years, widowed and divorced players are known to have found a new partner or companion in the intimacy of a foursome.

Bridge often provides an insight into a player's character. The way we play gives us away. There are the timid players who constantly underbid for fear of 'going down'; there are the wildly optimistic, who tend to overbid in an attempt to secure a game or rubber. Others will never find fault with their own game and always blame a missed contract on their partner. Members of a 'social' bridge club may politely suffer a player who at the end of each game will dissect it with post-speculative didacticism, if only to show off the quality of their memory. Equally tolerated in such a genteel atmosphere is the player who takes an eternity to decide which suit to bid or not to bid, or which card to lead or discard. As perhaps in other card or board games, conclusions may be drawn as to a player's temperament and the way he may conduct his life and relationships.

Bridge is a game of chance and skill, ideally assisted by a good memory. It may lead to serious addiction, allegedly even to an unhealthy obsession. For players thus hooked, the fun has surely gone out of their game, and fun ought to be a part of bridge when not played for stakes.

However, who would deny that at its casual end the game of chance and skill does not tone up the inner man and woman, thus acting like a mild drug?

In the many clubs in which high-standard duplicate bridge is played, the atmosphere is spiked with adrenaline. Attempts at conversation or comments on some aspect of play are taboo, and a less experienced player's apology for having let his partner down may well fall on stony silence or be met with caustic criticism in monosyllables. In contrast, 'social' rubber bridge clubs flourish in the country, because they provide fun and social interaction. No money changes hands, and when friendly matches are played, they do not make the less accomplished player perspire with anxiety. Slams may be rare, the rules of bidding not always be observed, but whatever a side's score, the pleasure of playing 'social' bridge is obvious: it is evident in the chatter between games, in the cries of delight whenever a player makes a trick with an unsuspected trump, or, despite a points deficit, manages to make a penalty-doubled contract. Nor will the other side point their guns at you should you through clever defensive play foil their contract. On the other hand, should YOU go down miserably, they have licence gleefully to applaud your defeat.

Apart from their dedication to the game and the mental stimulus it provides, casual players among the elderly usually welcome the chance to meet like-minded people. Indeed, the number of senior members of society, who indulge in their passion for bridge, is growing steadily. An added bonus is the opportunity for a chat during coffee breaks, the time to share someone's family news or air sentiments that will find listening ground.

I see a special benefit in 'social' bridge for the older player who lives alone or who is no longer able to be active in the community or pursue other interests. Such players do not only have their regular meetings to look forward to, but there is the need to organise their week. It is something to get up for in the morning, to get dressed and focus on two hours of play in congenial company. To feel they are not alone. To have a chance to laugh and sharpen the brain. Ultimately, to feel part of a bridge fraternity.

Allegedly, 1.2 million people in Britain play mainstream or Acol bridge, and their number is rising. Since its genesis, an entire bridge language has evolved, in which players communicate. Terms like Take-Out, Take-Out Double, Finesse, Weak or Strong Club, Stayman, Jumps, Overcall and Bids Pre-emptive, Cue or Forcing, Opening Threes and Twos, not to mention the Gerber or Blackwood Slam Conventions and other more advanced ploys and coups - such bridge-speak might easily deter a potential player, and bewilder a learner. However, once having mastered the basic rules of play, many novices soon become enthusiasts. Once a player, always a player, say the initiated, and it is no secret why the game holds its disciples in thrall: for whether an aficionado of the 'serious' or the 'social' game, the attraction of bridge lies in the combination of bid computation, intelligent play and the luck of cards. Whatever hand one holds, one requires discipline of thought and a good memory. And one never stops learning, for there is always room for improvement. Perhaps this is a challenge in itself.

Bridge is now being played on the Internet. But play through such a medium is potentially for loners hooked to the computer screen, or for non-working folk with money and plenty of time on their hands.

For me, the computer illiterate, the mode of such play would lack all the components present in club play. Internet wizards are likely to disagree. For them such 'impersonal' games might have equal immediacy and, even, intimacy.

The future of bridge seems to hold unlimited possibilities. With the mental stimuli of the game said to hone intellectual acumen and, in the elderly player, keep senility at a respectable distance, a future government might see a national advantage in making bridge mandatory in schools. They may institute bridge degree courses at universities, and at up-market interviews the ability to compute the chances of a game on a set number of points, or drive home a slam, may determine an applicant's chances.

And now, anyone for bridge? Come, put down the latest blockbuster novel, shut off the computer and let's stimulate our grey cells. Let's cut for partners, shuffle the cards, deal and start the bidding. Something tells me that today is the day when I shall be able to shoot a Grand Slam.

2003

AND THEN THE LIGHT WENT

Anyone who watched the sun's eclipse in August 1999 in its totality or near-totality will have been affected by this natural phenomenon according to their emotional or spiritual make-up, their professional or lay interest in the event. Some people might have given the disappearing sun no more than a guarded cursory glance; for others the spectacle might have been a non-event. However, for the majority of people privileged to watch a total eclipse in their lifetime, it would have been a special experience. Many had sought an early vantage point where the eclipse was expected to be visible in its totality. Astronomers and astrophysicists might have rated it only one of the highlights of their careers, while students of planetary behaviour and hobby star-gazers would have seen it as no less than an optical feast. Bible literates and devout Christians may have been uncomfortably reminded of the Revelation or the hour when Christ had died on the Cross; when according to the Scriptures the sun had darkened over Jerusalem and Calvary. Others may have wondered whether failing light might some day be the harbinger of a global cataclysm.

Today we believe that a total obscuration must have taken place, coinciding with the Crucifixion and with Christ's last breath. Ignorant of solar and lunar orbiting cycles, at the time the spectacle would have plunged many watchers into terror. They might have interpreted the disappearance of the sun as the wrath of God, if not as a confirmation that Jesus was indeed His son.

Apart from the fascination with which in the South-East of England I watched the dimming of the light in my garden and listened to the eerie silence around me, I could not help thinking of the global consequences should due to some cosmic or man-made catastrophe, the sun remain obliterated or never rise again, never give light again, never warm and sustain our planet.

Would a total lasting darkness engulf us or another biblical flood drown all things living? Would we eventually manage to kill each other off with the most sophisticated weapon systems, being motivated - as history has proved throughout the ages - by greed and a lust for power, if not by religious fanaticism and the sheer forces of evil? Perhaps a galloping world-wide plague might make short shrift of humanity, its strain resistant to any known antibiotics. Earthquakes, volcanic eruptions, fire spurting forth from every split in the soil, might bring death to man and beast. Or, quite feasibly to scientists, could an asteroid strike our planet, one so massive that it spun the earth out of its orbit?

For the love of conjecture, what would each of us do, or try to do, if we were told that the end of the world was imminent, and that neither atomic power, nor science's last resort, were capable of averting Zero Hour? Perhaps one or two hours of grace, to bid our farewells. Grains of time in which we would hear the clock ticking noisily. It is an intriguing, admittedly morbid, yet scientifically feasible scenario, one perhaps not entirely grown out of a doom-merchant's imagination. All the more so since allegedly some mind-blowing scientific experiment is now underway that would teach us how the universe began, but which may also blow up the planet by creating a black hole and tearing our earth apart. An experiment[1] intended to emulate the Big Bang and Genesis, the primordial soup - one that does not allow for fatal errors. Indeed, opponents of such a venture speak of the very real possibility that it could unleash a deadly chain reaction which would lead to the collapse of all matter in the universe. Fortunately, mankind's sudden or long-term extinction is still speculative, though entirely plausible. Meanwhile, it provides rich food for science fiction, hell-bent 'Green' campaigners and environmentalists.

---

[1] The Large Hadron Collider

A Church of England minister recently asked his Sunday morning congregation: 'What would each of you do, or try to do, if we were told that the world was coming to an end in, say, a few hours? How would you spend the remaining precious time?' A silence reigned. It was a subject few, if any, worshippers might have yet contemplated. It required, after all, depth and latitude of thinking, as well as a readiness to face imponderables.

I asked myself how I would rapidly come to terms with an approaching Armageddon. Now, assuming I were at home at the time (priorities might be different if I sat in a dentist's chair, were flying across the Atlantic or pushing a supermarket trolley), my first impulse would be to ring my family. However, since everyone in the country would try to do the same, the network would surely be overloaded and break down. Neither would the car be of much use, as millions of motorists would try and reach loved ones, thus bringing all traffic on roads and motorways to a standstill. So what would I do? What could I do? Clear thinking dissolving in emotional mayhem, I might do something totally irrational, such as watering my houseplants, finishing the sentence of a letter or taking the washing off the line. Perhaps I might brew myself a last cup of tea, or as one for whom an egg-cup full of alcohol spells inebriation, open my only bottle of wine - a celebratory vintage and present from a friend and connoisseur. I'd fill my rooms with high decibel sounds of Bach, gather family photos around me and - with the wine having taken off the sharp edges of angst and frustration - walk for the last time through my garden which for many years has imparted solace and inspiration, a green haven, in which green thoughts were born.

The thought of Time running through an hourglass would finally make me look in the New Testament for words appropriate for journeying towards the Cloud of Unknowing, as the late Malcolm Muggeridge used to phrase the Presence of the Almighty. I might say a simple prayer, waiting for my heart to stop thumping and peace to enter me. And if I could manage it, I'd try to confront that last fleeting minute with a smile. By amending Dylan Thomas' lines, I'd try my best to 'go gently into that good night', and not to 'rave against the dying of the light'. Such a last rite would surely require all my physical and spiritual energy.

But then, how can any of us really predict what we would do with that last hour, and to what extreme behaviour such knowledge might drive us?

In our lifetime such a scenario might happily still remain conjecture, an academic question that few people will give another thought. Yet the very brevity of our existence, and the very real possibility of an Armageddon, some cosmic disaster or whatever has the potential to exterminate mankind in the near or distant future, should make us resolve to fill each day with at least one 'hour of sixty minutes' worth of distance run.'

2008

IN PRAISE OF PRAISE

'Well played', said my bridge partner, a former match player who runs her own club. And later, 'I enjoyed playing with you.'

Now, why did my face broaden with a smile? Why did I feel a flutter of elation? Well, for no other reason than that I had been given a proverbial pat on the back. Having been out of the game for over twenty-five years, I had been rewarded with a few words of praise for months of. revision and for finally having achieved a commendable standard.

I daresay that most of us are rather mean when it comes to praising someone's feat, whatever its scale. Yet it costs so little, and it does not detract in any way from our own achievements or self-esteem to acknowledge a special effort, something perhaps accomplished against all odds or through single-minded application.

I am not advocating panegyrics, but only what ought to be a courtesy of the heart - words that aim to please and further encourage, and which do not seek to flatter or ask for anything in return.

Why then are most of us so reluctant openly to salute some praiseworthy deed? In some people such restraint may be self-consciousness, and social barrier, envy or simply laziness of the heart. Some may feel that paying someone a personal tribute might be interpreted as gratuitous or hiding an ulterior motive, or that none but the most meritorious accomplishments deserve words of acclaim.

Let's be honest: whatever our age, we thrive on praise. We lap it up like bears licking clean a honey pot. It makes us grow an inch, spurs us on or lifts us out of the quicksand of doubt, depression or a negative attitude. It is often a crutch for aged parents, lone people and anyone battling with illness or a disability.

They say praise is the best diet, being both balm and tonic. And whether it is the voice of love or friendship or official recognition, it will create flutters of happiness, moments of incandescence.

As with applauding an adult for a fine performance or brave effort, so praise will affect children. Here, 'Well done!' are magic words which act as a reward for a good mark at school, a well-rendered passage on an instrument or even a minor achievement on the sports field. They provide further stimulus and may lie in as unassuming an act as a child tidying up a toy-cluttered room without the lure of a sweet or the threat of punishment. Indeed, what pride will blossom in a toddler's face when a parent admires a drawing which, though it resembles a tangle of coloured wires, is meant to be a portrait of 'Mummy'.

Let's admit: we are often tight-lipped in the applause department; we are often too busy, thoughtless or lack the necessary empathy to make congratulatory noises where they would be in order. Perhaps we should remember that even a whisper, an appreciative smile, a 'Well done', comes in hard currency.

That is why I go in praise of praise. And who knows, at my bridge club I may get another pat on the back should I bid and make a decisive game or, bless the thought, even reach a bridge 'high' with a slam, doubled and redoubled.

2003

IDYLLS OF MEMORY

I was born a romantic. Life, however, thought otherwise and forced me over the years to adopt a realistic attitude towards what was happening to me and around me. At heart, however, and only airing itself publicly through my writing, I have remained unashamedly romantic. Sometimes, certain sights, something I might read or hear, will trigger a romantic ride into the past. At other times, whenever life appears to have grown stale, or I have to stem nostalgia against the power or pain and loneliness, I retrieve some idyll of the past at will. There is no question that such heart-warming cameos have a therapeutic effect. They also make me realise that I am privileged to have a reservoir of memories which, whether being recalled or sparked off, will take me momentarily out of my shell. Perhaps that is why I celebrate beauty wherever I perceive it, whether in nature, music, the visual arts or the written word. In the still life of my summer garden, a romantic mood comes with the added premium of peace, a peace that is dropping slowly like a veil, taking the breath out of my cares.

It is thus on a fine summer morning that I step into the garden, a mug of tea in my hand, and my heart rejoices. There is not a single cloud in the sky and the air is still crisp. Not even a breeze is fondling the majestic willow tree, and since it is not shedding any leaves, the lawn looks like a smooth quality carpet. The roses are in bud, the first poppies squeeze their crimson colour through my plot of wildflowers and the lavender promises a much-loved scent. Apart from the sing-song of the resident bird population, no man-made sound invades the peace and stillness of the hour. For aeons of time, the world slips out of focus, the mind frames what it wants to retain - another idyll of memory perhaps to be retrieved on a bleak winter's day.

With great joy I recall the Edenic panorama of the Heiligensee in Potsdam, the lake on which as a sixteen year-old schoolgirl I spent many a hot summer afternoon in a dinghy. The memory of this serene lake, over which the heat haze seemed to have been shot through with magic, has never left me.

As during the summer of 1943 the war was closing in on Germany, and every night the sky to the east coloured red from the fire-bombing on Berlin, life for me was the sum of wailing sirens, meagre rations and page-long obituaries. At school, it was anti-Jewish propaganda, endless Heil Hitler greetings and Party-orientated lessons. On the streets, soldiers, Swastika banners, marching columns, life-sized pictures of Hitler and posters boosting morale sated the eyes, while in its Big Brother role, the Hitler Youth commanded obedience and political loyalty. With the future a closed book for me, but for the prospect of compulsory war service, my afternoons on the lake transcended the war. They made me live as in another space or time. They conveyed to me a world, in which beauty and tranquillity acted as a balm and an opiate.

The lake, as I wrote in The Naked Years, was mine that summer:

'No other boats intruded on its idyll, no human voices pierced its calm, while the lazy passage of the boat, and the swans and ducklings which never ventured far from the bullrushes, caused no more than a slight agitation of the water.

Rowing and drifting through the heat haze, watching and marvelling. Fish jumping for midges, minnows weaving about in emerald water, gauze-winged dragonflies hovering and darting in pursuit of prey. Watching and marvelling, before manoeuvring the boat through a cascade of weeping willows into a tiny bay, where the water laps placidly against its bows.

Here then, the afternoon is complete: on the bank, forget-me-nots, marigolds and wild irises; on the water, the lush green plates of floating duckweed; above me, sunshine streaking through the skirt of plying branches, creating a crocheted pattern of light. A scent of jasmine, a water-vole diving into the water, a startled warbler escaping to a higher branch… time too languid to move, low-keyed afternoon sounds attuned to sun-drenched tranquillity.

Later, when the sun is about to set behind the century-old trees in the park, it is time to row over to the small island at the far end of the lake, to take off my swimsuit and glide into the water from a hidden inlet.

The warm velvety water caresses my body, makes my breasts swell. And in the ecstasy of swimming in tune above water through the last burnishing shafts of light, or submerged, with my eyes trying to penetrate the aquarium world of fish and quivering, writhing pondweed, I wish I could store time in a glass jar like seashells or marbles.'

It is quite remarkable how facilely and in fine detail memory can retrieve similar scenes; how, over the years, though their colours may have faded, nothing of what had made them memorable has been lost. I believe that given the right conditions, anyone with heightened sensibilities may slip back into some special landmarked space of the past, hearing, seeing and feeling again what was once a cherished reality.

I can think of many other scenes which have remained vibrant in my memory: the view across Hong Kong Harbour at night or, under a full moon, from the top of Lantao's highest mountain across the China Sea; a deserted golden-sand beach on as yet tourist-free Mallorca. Pine-scented forest paths in the Silesian Riesengebirge, leading past gurgling brooks and blueberry carpets, or the luscious gardens of the Villa Carlotta on Lake Como. In The Alien Years, I remember with an acute sense of nostalgia a sandy cove on the north-eastern coast of Mallorca, reached through a cleft between steep overhanging cliffs, and on a track no wider than a man's shoulders. Having found the narrow entrance, my friend and I felt like children who had come across a secret door to fairyland. Enchanted, we penetrated deeper into the majestic world of sea-buffeted, sea-shaped diluvian rocks.

> 'Suddenly, light, echoes, a transparent sea-water pool awash with sunbeams. A bed of smooth, disk-like pebbles visible as through a magnifying glass.
>
> We took our clothes off and gingerly stepped into the water in which to wear a swimsuit would have been a sacrilege. And the magic of the place was such that we bathed in silence, picking up pebbles and running them through our fingers like pearls. Or floating on our backs, eyes closed... Or diving, eyes open, through a world of liquid glass, like fish, like water nymphs...'

Now and then I flip through the pages of glossy travel magazines which exalt the pleasures of cruising. I journey back in memory to the early Sixties, when my young family and I sailed to Hong Kong on a small cargo boat. There may be a few 'banana boat' passages still available in some parts of the world today, but in our packaged and entertainment-oriented holiday industry, cruise ships often carry more than a thousand passengers. None of these liners can possibly offer the same quality of experiences.

Then, our vessel was a mere speck on the oceans, and we shared it with only a few passengers and crew. One could hear the waves lapping against the hull. One could stare across calm waters with no more than the muted drone of the ship's engine for background sound. And on deck, on a moonlit night, one could easily lose oneself in the wide southern skies.

In A Slow Boat To Hong Kong, I recalled:

> 'constellations not seen in our northern hemisphere, stars shining so brightly over the silver-ribbed sea and the dimly-lit deck, as to make me feel infinitely small, a mere microcosm of the universe. I would become a child, a dreamer, a philosopher, a lonely human being confronted with the Infinitum of Space.'

One short-lived experience still flashes through my mind at odd times: a swim in the yellowish, lukewarm waters of the Suez Canal in sizzling heat in 1961. What I photographed in my mind was the sun setting over the Arabian desert like a blood orange, while silhouetted against it in picture-book style, a caravan was moving slowly along its western banks. It made me think of all the stories I had read about the Arabian desert, and about some fearless, single-minded explorers and Victorian travellers who had braved hardship, ever-present thirst and long marches though arid wastes under a blistering sun. I thought of how they had pitched their tents at night, drunk tea with Bedouins or slept next to their camels under a diamantine sky, enwrapped by an all-pervading silence, which was perhaps broken now and again by an Arab's snore, the bark or rustle of a camel.

There were times when I stood on Florence's Ponte Vecchio at sunset, admiring the striking scene before me, one which I would later incorporate in The Deluge:

'The sun was injecting flaming streaks of light into the sluggish green waters of the Arno, bathing the roof-tops, turrets and domes of Florence in a soft, rosy haze, thus mellowing or diffusing their outline. In a world of my own, the centuries receded. I thought of the great masters of the Renaissance, who had made Florence a Mecca of art and literature; of the poets and scribes who had once stood on the famous bridge at sunset like myself, marvelling at the blushing of the city at the close of day, or seeking inspiration. Perhaps Dante had once leaned on the same parapet, gazing at all this rosiness and the softness of contours, whilst shaping in his mind new immortal lines for La Vita Nuova. Or Byron...'

There are many more memories like these, and I treasure them like priceless paintings. For few are the places nowadays, where enchantment can reign supreme. Man, motor-cars, property developers and mass tourism have all too often ravaged their tranquillity and virginity. Many, on the other hand, are accessible only to the wealthy and the exclusive order of our society.

As for me, who is dependent on medication, temperate climes and a modicum of creature comforts, I must be content with the idylls of memory and the green pleasures of my garden.

ART, RELICS AND SENSIBILITIES

In my lifetime I have wandered through many an art gallery, museum and special exhibition. Some of the paintings, relics and artefacts have remained indelibly in my memory. Some stirred my emotions like wind forking through a harp, some stimulated my imagination or just appealed to my sense of beauty, colour and shape. And there were those which sent the odd goose pimple down my spine, as they confirmed or substantiated what we know about the life of Christ, or what shed further light on that of the early Christians.

Throughout the centuries, Western artists have celebrated their faith on canvas, in stone, bronze and silver; they have created frescoes and tapestries or left their immortal legacy in churches, just as writers left theirs on parchment and in books.

Many are the works of art which have touched a chord inside me. I remember some paintings at the Louvre holding me spellbound at a time when I still knew little about the world of art. When I finally acquired some knowledge, I was richer for the experience. In the Uffizi, I thus found romantic and spiritual beauty in Titian's *Flora*, the painting famous for its exultant intensity of colour. Botticelli's *Primavera* aroused my admiration, as did many other masterpieces which I saw on canvas for the first time. Still in Florence, Michaelangelo's *Piétà* played quietly on my emotions, while in the Green Cloisters of the Santa Maria Novella Church, I marvelled at Uccello's fresco *Il Diluvio*, depicting Noah's Ark, the terrors of the biblical flood and God's Covenant, a theme on which I later based my first three-dimensional novel *The Deluge*. As before an altar, I stood at the foot of Cimabue's *Crucifix*, the most dramatic work of art produced in the Middle Ages. At that very moment a solitary sunbeam settled on the crucified Jesus and the gilt-flaked Cross, which lent the scene an awesome, yet comforting immediacy.

In Berlin a few years ago, at the Charlottenburger Schloss, I viewed a special exhibition of the most prominent paintings of the German Romantic school, among them those by Adolph Menzel, Moritz Schwind and Caspar David Friedrich. Friedrich's landscapes, of which most are unashamedly romantic, included one which evoked in me an image of war-time desolation: a cold winter morning in Berlin, following a heavy night-time air raid, with the sun rising like a fireball. In the foreground, starkly silhouetted against the horizon and a snow-covered landscape, a ravaged tree, its amputated branches groping towards the sky as in a silent accusation.

One painting by Menzel had a nostalgic effect on me: *The Flute Concert*, showing King Frederick The Great of Prussia playing the flute at a musical soirée in the palace of Sanssouci. Painted in gorgeous Titianesque colours, it reminded me of the splendid gilt-framed print which used to hang over the grand piano on my grandmother's drawing room. Unlike Gainsborough's *Blue Boy* which became the victim of silver fish, Menzel's masterpiece changed hands in the winter of 1944/45 for half a pound of butter and an egg.

An exhibition of Monet's paintings in Berlin's National Gallery not long ago, and coinciding with my visit to the city, allowed me to view his *Water Lilies* in the original. In the restored part of the Kaiser-Friedrich Memorial Church, I came across a poignant reminder of the last war: a Cross made of pieces of shrapnel and nails from the bomb-ravished Coventry Cathedral, and given to the Church by the English congregation as a gesture of forgiveness and reconciliation.

The privilege of seeing the painted limestone portrait of Queen Nefertiti, sculpted by a BC Egyptian artist, also stands out in my memory. With her pure profile and slender neck, she symbolised female beauty of her time. As a young woman I had a chance to see the famous 15th century Riemenschneider *Altar*, in which the artist used powerful Gothic symbols to express his intense religiosity. In later years I often lost myself in some 'golden age' or Arcadian scene on canvas, as depicted by Turner and earlier landscape artists.

Many masterpieces I should still like to see: da Vinci's *Last Supper*, the Sistine Chapel, Rodin's *The Kiss*, Gainsborough's *Blue Boy* and many other works of art, just as I should like to go on a cultural pilgrimage to the Terracotta Army, the Pyramids, Rameses' Temple, the Blue Mosque and Ayers Rock, marvel at the golden mask of the pharaoh Tutankhamun, and other wonders of the world.

While I am not, and never shall be, an expert on visual art, I am fortunate in that I have sensibilities that allow me to admire, gain pleasure from, or feel touched by secular paintings which represent the world as we know it, and as generations before us have known it. However, perhaps in unison with other Christians of solid or fluctuating faith, I always feel very brittle inside when I stand face to face with paintings, relics and artefacts which are witness to the Christian faith since biblical times. And like myself, all but the most rigid sceptics and confirmed atheists must surely have felt a tingle of emotion on reading that the face of Jesus had recently been discovered on the wall of a Norman church like the alleged image on the Turin Shroud or Saint Veronica's Veil, whether or not this latest claim should prove to be an optical illusion or the behaviour of ageing stonework. For no one really knows what Jesus Christ looked like. Yet, oh, how much would we like to know.

We may hope, even cry out, for evidence - other than documented in the Scriptures - that there is a God and a Holy Spirit; we may forever look for Christ's footsteps to take us through His life, His suffering, Crucifixion and Ascension. And pending that revelation, except through faith, we may come to see in the religious art of two centuries a confirmation of our own belief, the powerful counterbalance to our increasingly agnostic society; we may acknowledge the trend of people turning away from the Church as an institution which not only clings to antiquated rituals and canon laws, but also tries in vain to shake off the image of the Inquisition, the burning of infidels and heretics, crimes for which the aged Pope - in an unprecedented public confession - asked for forgiveness on behalf of the Catholic Church.

The fact that modern art seldom, if at all, expresses faith or religious images, invites food for thought. One does not need the perspicacity of Cardinal Giacomo Biffi, the contender to the papal throne, nor the Cassandra voices of lesser church leaders, to realise that the Antichrist is 'walking among us'. According to the Cardinal, Satan is not the beast with seven heads, as described in the Book of Revelation, but a fascinating personality who deceives and corrupts by promoting vague and fashionable ideas and values. He is, I daresay, by nature an enemy of religious art and would wish to destroy all the masterpieces which glorify the image of Christ.

Yet although godlessness now seems to be *en vogue*, many people still attend church services; many couples get married in church and have their children baptised and confirmed. Others keep their personalised faith in a closet or let their actions proclaim a Christian spirit. And in great numbers they are still visiting galleries and special exhibitions where religious art celebrates the best in Christianity.

A few years ago I saw an exhibition of the Dead Sea Scrolls, the most important archaeological find in modern times. Apart from two thousand year-old Aramaic scrolls, which contain the Books of the Hebrew Bible (the Christian Old Testament), there was a display of limestone pottery, inkwells, a hoard of silver coins, leather sandals, urns and other well-preserved objects which revealed the daily life and ownership of the pious Essene sect, and imparted a sense of religious history.

In one scroll fragment, the writer refers to a 'pierced' (crucified) Messiah; another caused a prayer-like silence among viewers: the metre-long Hebrew script which preserved the divine words of God given to Moses on Mount Sinai. It was a unique exhibition, to which people had come even from abroad. Just as in the spring of the new millennium in London, people flocked to the National Gallery's special exhibition 'Seeing Salvation - Images of Christ'.

Indeed, like pilgrims they came: backpackers, pensioners, men and women with an hour to spare between desks and computers; people in wheelchairs, teachers with reverential or open-minded sixth-formers in tow. While being of undisputed interest to clerics and theologians, the representation of Christ, his life and death in paintings and religious artefacts seemed to attract not only devout Christians and those of wavering or non-faith, but also adherents of other religions. For where else could one see - so the atmosphere suggested - 'the greatest story ever told' immortalised in stone, bronze and scrolls?

Among other notable religious paintings, two stand out for me: Salvador Dali's *Christ of St John of the Cross*, the impressive Surrealist picture which is said to reflect the fascination and disaffection with 20th century Christianity. The contrast of colours and outer-space perspective appeal both to my intellect and, symbolically, to my faith. On the other hand, *The Light of the World*, by William Holman Hunt, claims to be the most celebrated image of Christ. His face is beautifully lit as from within, and its expression conveys spiritual love, understanding and forgiveness. It fascinated me. It spoke to me. Indeed, it seemed to speak to onlookers in one common language, regardless of nationality or faith.

At the National Gallery that day, I meandered through rooms teeming with the works of Zubarán, Donatello, El Greco, Titian, Bellini and Velázquez, and I could not help musing about modern Christianity which now is often described as 'uncool' and out of step with our secular age. Dissenting voices will maintain that it is not in decline - despite the falling numbers of church-goers. Indeed, judging by the number of visitors to this exhibition, which was hailed as London's celebration of the new Millennium, faith would appear still to be a reckonable element in our society. There may also exist a growing tendency of agnostics to search for a spiritual icon, for something that feeds the soul.

One has to accept that many people - as Ludovic Kennedy put it so succinctly, are saying 'Goodbye, God, we can live without you.' But can we afford to bid God goodbye and altogether dispense with religion as our moral and spiritual framework, because secular idolatry allows us more leeway in out thoughts and actions? The crowds flocking to the London exhibition would seem to prove otherwise.

Many people have indeed shown God the front door in our time, and many will continue to do so in years to come, but who knows how many will want to re-admit Him through the back door, when they find that the state of society and a de-humanising technology are draining them of sensibilities and, ultimately, of what transcends our non-spiritual world?

2003

WHAT WAS IT LIKE?
or
Epitaph for my grandmother

My maternal grandmother starved to death in Berlin in 1946 at the age of sixty-three. She died of gastric ulcers which would finally no longer pass food, least of all the stodgy maize bread and the basic cabbage diet of the famine years of 1945 and '46 in Germany. Berlin being occupied by Russian and Allied Forces, and medical facilities for Germans virtually non-existent, there were no hospital beds for civilians, no surgeons to operate, and no medication to halt the progress of a gastric stricture. This, ultimately, led to a slow death by starvation. My grandmother's last meal, my mother told me, had been a beaten egg, exchanged on the black market for the last of her Roman goblets - just one of many prized possessions traded in for a few grams of butter, sugar or flour in order to boost the hunger rations of the time. Apparently, in her last moments she had spoken of me, her favourite grand-daughter, for whom she had often provided a weekend or school holiday refuge while I was growing up at a children's home in Potsdam.

As refugees during the arctic winter of '45, we had been sharing a tiny, unheated attic room in a small West German town; together we had lived through the local breakdown of law and order, before watching from a cellar window the invasion of Sherman tanks and the door-to-door fighting of American troops. And just before the country's capitulation, when the local German population was temporarily 'evacuated' to the countryside by order of the US 'commandant', to enable the French and Belgian forced labourers to loot residents' houses, fit themselves out and take whatever they fancied, my grandmother and I joined the enforced exodus, finding shelter in a farmer's barn. Here, this refined lady had to endure the indignity of bedding down on a byre's hay for several nights and having to drink from, and wash under, the farmyard pump.

She winced before squatting over a hastily dug latrine in the field, and clumsily ladled from a tin the watery cabbage soup which an American officer had ordered the farmer's wife to cook for the 'refugees'.

For me, at the age of nineteen, having already coped with worse, often life-threatening, situations with the survival spirit of youth, our compulsory encampment held memories of Hitler Youth camps in some Eastern outbacks. My grandmother, on the other hand, was coping with the tail end of the war with a stoic acceptance, never moaning and bravely falling in with the farmyard routine. Picking straw from her hair and smoothing her dress, she was as visibly imperturbable as on the last train out of Berlin earlier that year when people, packed rigidly up to the compartment ceilings, were choking for air and urinating where they sat, stood or clung. Hell could not have been worse...

When we were finally allowed to return to the burgled medieval town, finding most of our few clothes and possessions gone, she proclaimed resignedly, 'Well, at least they have left me my corset and hair-waving tongs.'

In time she would return to Berlin and the debris of her former life, while I was trying to survive elsewhere in the British Zone. Yet not before a shaky postal service between the Russian and Western Zones of Occupation had started up again did I hear of her all too early demise. I recall an overwhelming sense of loss. Of frustration. Of anger at the Russian zonal sovereignty which still barred German civilians from crossing the arbitrarily staked border, even if only to reunite with surviving family members or visit the graves of loved ones.

May a brief portrait of my grandmother thus form a fond memorial:

My grandmother was born in 1876 and educated in the then French Alsace. I remember her as a model of understated elegance and sophistication, a guardian also of tradition and middle-class values. Interestingly, her German never denied her French-Alsatian upbringing, and thus my mother and I subliminally adopted some French words, many of which had also been brought into Germany by Huguenot refugees in the 17th century. To this day, terms like *chaiselongue* (sofa), *portières* (heavy curtains), *buffet* (sideboard) and *plumeau* (feather bed), to name but a few, still slip into my own vocabulary.

Married to an Alsatian umbrella manufacturer and Berlin company director, who died in the early Twenties, my grandmother was blessed with the kind of money that allowed her to enjoy a comfortable lifestyle, which included the services of a live-in maid, a manicurist, coiffeur, dressmaker, and milliner, and subscriptions to the Berlin Philharmonic and State Opera. An avid lover of classical music, she introduced me to Beethoven and Brahms symphonies, and to concerts conducted by the celebrated Wilhelm Furtwängler, the musical morale-booster of Berlin, who even during air raids would not lay down his baton when the macabre thump of bombs falling all around the house joined the beat of percussion instruments or formed an uneasy background to some lofty symphonic strains.

I recall family luncheons at her home before the war, at which I enjoyed roast goose with dumplings or whole carp cooked *bleu*, at the same time taking in the sight of fine table linen, silver and crystal - visual lessons in cultured dining which left an imprint on my perception of prandial sophistication.

I also remember her as an accomplished cook. It was she who taught me how to prepare a *sauce béchamel, haute cuisine* mashed potatoes and vegetables *à la française*. When jam-making, she would allow me to stir the bubbling fruit in a copper kettle and - for the traditional *streussel* or apple cake - to crack the eggs and blend them into the dough.

And I still see her setting out for a stroll or shopping spree on Berlin's legendary Kurfürstendamm, wearing some discreet finery and, as a lady of her class, the mandatory accessories of pearls, hat and gloves.

There was also a mystery in my grandmother's life, a romantic episode that may have ended in response to the moral dictates of the time. For whenever there rose the strains of *Der Rosenkavalier* on the radio, she would go all misty-eyed and her face would light up from within.

Being of a gentle disposition, and loved by her family, I shall always remember her as the epitome of respectability and grace. Yet, when it mattered, when substantial financial, personal and material loss - if not the great social leveller of the war - required her to adapt to a changed lifestyle, she did so without a whine and with a fatalistic attitude. Whatever I learned from her, and ultimately from my mother, I have tried to hand down to my children like an inheritance of spirit, manners and tradition - a mirror of the past.

If only, while there was still time, I had asked her 'What was it like, growing up at the turn of the century? What was school like? How did you meet my grandfather?'

What was it like? Alas, questions asked too late.

GOING BACK

As we are moving into our dotage, many of us will be disinclined to look the future squarely in the face, speculating about the quality of our remaining years and their terminal point. Many of us will agree that this is quite a natural human tendency. Yet, as we are watching the boldly marked, tapering perspective of our life ahead, some elderly folk will delight in going back in time as sight-seeing tourists. They will visit places that once formed important personal landmarks or where they had pivotal experiences.

In the *perpetuum mobile* of Time, our past is forever lost, but it is not dead. It remains part of us. We cannot shake some of it off, add to it, change it or cut out undesirable chunks. Some of us may be dragging memories along like an incubus, others might see a retrospective as a self-flagellating exercise. However, most of us will cling to what in the hinterland of our past stands out as a pristine landscape - something that still has the power to cuddle the soul and raise a smile.

For many elderly people still in good physical shape, travel even to a far corner of the world no longer presents an obstacle. They may wish to re-visit the premises of their childhood or formative years, or places where they once felt gloriously alive. They may venture to a location still echoing of war and death and suffering, only to luxuriate in a feeling of gratitude to have survived. Then again, a venue reminiscent of some roguish and devil-may-care years may imbue a sense of how successfully one has outgrown one's former self.

Yet popular advice is never to go back where the heart still dwells, for all too often new impressions superimpose themselves on happy sepia images of the mind, thus tarnishing original recall or altering it beyond recognition. Time will have eaten away substance; it will have allowed nature to take over or have redesigned the playing fields of our youth. It might be the garden, in which we used to dream of fairies or play hide-

and-seek, which is now overgrown, its trees cut down and gravel replacing the once manicured lawn. Paths, along which we used to ride our bikes, may have disappeared under new housing schemes, motorways criss-cross the familiar landscape that once impelled local artists to paint. All of which will leave us with a lump in the throat, making us conscious of the rape of memories.

Rare, indeed, are the occasions when we find that nothing has visibly changed in a place where we played hopscotch, discovered the other sex or battled with the demands of adulthood. After all, nothing in life remains static, and we know that its constant flux is no guardian of what was once part of us.

A rendezvous with the past always has the quality of a two-edged sword: we may come away smiling, intrigued or pleased with our encounters, or we may bleed a little inside, feeling like mourners returning from a funeral. Whichsoever, we shall have experienced something that does not favour a repetition, something that will not release the same thrills twice. I know. For I have played the 'Going Back' game myself several times, out of curiosity or nostalgia, if not in order to lay to rest memories that do not deserve a recall.

Shortly after the Berlin Wall came down, I visited both East Berlin and the former DDR. I went back to Potsdam, Frederick The Great's garrison town and crib of Prussian militarism, where I had spent nine crucial years of my life at school, in a private girls' home and in bedsits.

The side street leading up to the home symbolised the degree to which all private and most public buildings had been allowed to decay after the war. The pavement resembled an assault course, its holes liable to cause a sprained ankle to any pedestrian who did not keep his nose to the ground. The façades of grand villas, some of which, turreted and architectural showpieces of Kaiser's time, were still pockmarked from gun shots, often exposing the steel supports of balconies and shell-vandalised stucco work. The chestnut trees which once lined the road had never been trimmed since the outbreak of war, and now formed a giant jungle canopy over it. The former home, a splendid 19th century villa which, following the zonal division of Germany, had been taken over by the headquarters of the local (SED) Communist Party, showed blatant neglect. Its wooden fence and gate were broken, windows were opaque with grime, and what had once been a lovely garden with a lawn, flowerbeds and a swing and see-saw area, had not only been used for forty-five years as a parking lot, but also as a coke dump. The large veranda, on which we, the young inmates, were allowed to sleep on sultry August nights, when a full moon and a myriad of stars formed a planetarium-like sky, was now a scramble of broken glass, steel bars and detritus. It was obvious that the Cold War occupants had reigned on the premises just as Russian soldiers and the families had done in private German homes during the years of occupation: with no respect for property and cultured surroundings.

Sadly I turned away, desperately trying to hold on to a part of my childhood which had brought out in me qualities that would later stand me in good stead.

Continuing on my way that morning, I walked down to the banks of the Heiligensee, 'my' dream-like lake of one hot summer, whose images I had preserved like priceless fossils. But on this cold and grey day in March its waters were dark and restless, and under the overhanging branches of willows and elders, a forbidding black.

I visited my old school, which I remembered with its swastika flag flying proudly in front of the main entrance. Its basement windows had been bricked up during the war years, to protect pupils from bomb blasts and flying shrapnel. The building was in a sorry state of repair. It looked deserted. I located the janitor who, short of rolling out the red carpet for the former schoolgirl and visitor from England, explained that since Reunification most schools in the former DDR were still closed, awaiting Bonn's new educational directives.

Entering what for many years had been my classroom, I gaped with disbelief: the desks, now devoid of their sunken inkpots and abominably scratched by leagues of bored girls, stood in the same order they had in the early Forties. I half expected our maths teacher to scrawl algebraic symbols on the blackboard or throw a piece of chalk at some inattentive soul. I sat down at 'my' desk near the window, through which during lessons I had watched the antics of starlings and the drift of clouds, while planning the afternoon's leisure activities...

How facilely a receptive mind can step back in time.

The experience repeated itself in the school yard in which during the Hitler years an area had been used for sports and team games. Miraculously, its long- and high-jump pit was still *in situ*, though the once beach-like sand now looked like dumped cement. What, however, marked the passage of time for me most bizarrely, was the wooden board, from which I, the future athlete, had reached long-jump lengths never recorded by the school before. Now reduced in size, it looked weather-beaten and too rutted to support even a child's foot.

A visit to Potsdam would not have been complete without paying my respects to the familiar sights of Sanssouci Park, and without allowing myself a few minutes of bitter-sweet nostalgia at the Chinese Tea Pavilion. For here, my first love, a young Panzercorps Lieutenant, had kissed me, the blithely innocent sixteen year-old schoolgirl, with a gentleness that held all the futility of war, if not a premonition that before long he would be killed at the Russian front. Needless to say, as I remembered the world dissolving around me at the time, my arthritic frame cast off the years as lightly as a tree its leaves during an autumn gale.

Over the years I went back to other places which delineated my progression in life. In some, I experienced neither positive nor negative emotions, in others a flush of gratitude that I had come through some particular testing or life-threatening ordeals with my body, mind and integrity still intact. I might even feel a sense of pride, at having coped with the demands made upon me.

Sometimes my senses heightened an encounter. Thus, in a disused corridor of the former Oxford Infirmary - whose wooden floor I had scrubbed, waxed and polished in 1948 on my knees - I heard my coarse brush scouring the soft-soaped boards to the verse-rhythm of the 'Lady of Shallot', and the bumper screeching with every move. Walking through an empty ward of the former Warnford (Oxford) Mental Hospital, which held audible memories from my psychiatric nursing days, the clamouring voices of deranged patients all but drowned my footsteps.

While I revisited some of the wards at King Edward's Hospital in Windsor, where I had spent three years of general nursing training, I seemed to hear the clanging of the metal bedpans and the squealing of the surgical trolley wheels. I smelt Lysol and saw Matron sternly checking bedside lockers for motes of dust, and running her eyes down the row of beds in the hope, no doubt, of finding some crease or unhappy fold. I saw myself on night duty by the light of a dim desk lamp, facing the ghostly or all too real sounds of a nocturnal ward.

In Cala Major on Mallorca, I looked in vain for the picturesque villa and garden which had been my home for nine months in the early Fifties. Now, slum-like blocks of flats spread along the concrete path and up the hill, and the once intimate beach at its foot was alive with noisy bars, trashy shops and half-naked tourists.

In contrast, in Berlin I once went back to the detached house in which I had seen my three sons growing up - to the years when they had looked for Easter eggs and chocolate bunnies behind trees and daffodils. The city in which in winter they went skiing and sledging on the Teufelsberg with Mum in tow, and in summer would peg their tent in the garden and feast on sausages and baked beans like campers. The house looked somewhat smaller and the roadside linden trees had grown to a stately size. Otherwise nothing appeared to have changed: images beautifully preserved, allowing total recall.

A string of other places, both in England and abroad, to which I went back out of curiosity or to indulge in nostalgia, conveyed to me the huge learning and maturing process I had undergone. Sometimes I was marvelling: had that really been me, that insecure, vulnerable, trusting and often imprudent fledgling of a pretty girl with her irrepressible spirit and romantic yearnings? She who at an early age had lived through what for some people is the stuff of a lifetime?

Life, as my various return visits had endorsed, had indeed been a stern taskmaster. It had sawn off and polished the rough edges of my personality, while multi-coloured experiences had spawned worldly wisdom.

I no longer play the going-back game. Whatever hostile spirits used to hang around some places of my early past, the luminosity of some of my later years has long exorcised them. And as for walking in the green gardens of my life, I do not have to go back to where they were laid out. Their flowers are in bloom all the year round, knowing no season.

2005/8

THE CHEQUERED BOARD OF DESTINY

'There was a door to which I found no key,
There was a veil past which I could not see'

(Omar Khayyám)

I have always been intrigued by the question of whether or not, from the moment we are born, the lives of each of us are firmly tied to a pre-ordained pattern. It is an enigma which refuses to be solved.

The power which presides over our fortunes, and which is the end and purpose to which we are assigned, has been given many names: Destiny, Fate, Providence, God's Will, Kismet, Nemesis, Schicksal and, more popularly, One's Stars or What is Written in the Cards. Philosophers and many writers have tried to analyse what most likely has been written into our Book of Life the moment we enter this world. Novelists have dealt with a character's attempt to change the course of a specific event, in order to escape or alter its consequences. Similarly, historians have speculated on how the course of history would have changed, if by virtue of a different political decision or military strategy, or certain inciting agents, the two World Wars had been avoided: indeed, if the assassination attempts on Hitler had been successful. It is an interesting conjecture. Yet for many people venturing into the high altitudes of hypothetical and esoteric subjects, the question remains whether every incident in our life is irredeemable, in the sense that we have passively to accept what promises to have a negative impact on our affairs; or whether we have been given some leeway to change, here and there, the path of our destiny, by forestalling what would appear to be a preordained incident, or by controlling some of its sequential issues.

In novels the fictional manipulation of Destiny makes for a fascinating read, but it will remain no more than fantasy. The in-depth manoeuvring of philosophers and historians does, however, give much food for thought to those inclined to look farther than their visible horizon. It is impossible to compute the array of interlocking events should something in our life suddenly fall out of place or act like a stick thrown into its spokes. Plans may have gone wrong, relationships foundered, or we my have suffered any of the serious setbacks to which many of us are destined. We may feel resentful towards our *karma*, dispirited, angry with ourselves or with others, ignorant as we still are of the purpose behind it. Yet everything that happens to us does so for a reason, so philosophers and theologians declare, and often enough the future bears this out.

In his Rubaiyát, Omar Khayyám speaks of the chequered board where 'Destiny with Man for pieces plays'. William Cowper defines Destiny as the force which, like God, moves in a mysterious way. Friedrich Nietzsche, the German philosopher, on the other hand, is more pragmatic. For him 'the future makes the laws which govern our today'.

Whereas I do not argue that man is being moved around on the Board of Destiny like a chess piece, I am inclined to ascribe several potentially fatal or far-reaching incidents in my own life, which I miraculously survived or side-stepped, to being shunted around by a Higher Authority, if not to being part of a script that was put into my crib. Yet I also hold with Philip Wylie's tenet that 'Man's Destiny lies half with himself and half without'.

While a fool will always blame an ill constellation of his stars for personal failure, and for every mishap he could have avoided had he acted more circumspectly, and while every confirmed fatalist will always accept meekly whatever blow Life, Fate or an 'uncaring God' delivers to him, others will try and manoeuvre its consequences into acceptable channels. They will attempt to change what is changeable. We may not be able to avert strokes of ill-luck or whatever hostile scenario we are being presented with, but with prudence we may handle its progression.

I always held dear the following prayer-lines attributed to an eighteenth century German theologian: 'God grant me the serenity to accept the things I cannot change/the courage to change the things I can/and the wisdom to know the difference.'

In order to know the difference we need power of judgement and maturity of thought. Both are, I believe, the sum of knowledge and experience, wisdom that comes to those who remain eager pupils in life's ongoing teaching process, and - as Mark Twain puts it - to those who are patient.

In facing a new situation, perhaps it all boils down to accepting it bravely, making adjustments, redesigning plans, coming to terms with personal loss or failure, or re-assessing a relationship. In this, each of us will cope according to his ability and circumstances. We may be powerless to avert the proverbial 'slings and arrows of outrageous fortune', but with every effort we make in dealing with whatever has bruised our souls or thrown a boulder into our path, and with every judicious attempt to tailor consequences to our needs, we will grow stronger. We shall, ultimately, acquire the wisdom to confront our destiny as philosophers or challengers, as the case may be.

When we have reached an age in which through the decline of mobility and mental acumen our life is staked more narrowly, we may be more frequently subjected to the miasmal wiles of life. We might pick up a stray virus, trip over a loose stone or through negligence provoke a domestic accident. Then again, we may have to battle with ill-health or a disability which further reduces the range and quality of our lives. Fortunately, however, a large percentage of senior members of our society would seem to be able to pass their remaining years in the more uneventful and often very enjoyable realms of old age.

Life, as we know, is a long train of events which are often inter-connected. Trivial causes may give rise to monumental effects. Yet we often do not realise that when one door closes on us, another will open. Nor is it sometimes immediately obvious that what we blame on a hostile fate is in fact a kind act of Providence.

My own life was saved on several occasions by what some people would call 'good luck'. But what is 'good luck'? Is it a gift from heaven or something to which one is predestined? Christians will speak of a Divine Blessing or Intervention, philosophers see in it destiny's wilful or purposeful move on the chequered board. Now, many years later, I see a pattern in it all: I realise that I had to suffer some drastic personal blows, endure physical pain and loneliness, in order to think and feel the way I do and, ultimately, to have become what I am. Whatever flings of joy and happiness I was granted on the way were, I believe, intended to restore a balance. For me, destiny is not so much a 'board-player' as a puppet-master, the Higher Power of so many names, who acts as scriptwriter and director of man's show on earth. Destiny will always remain the enigma wrapped in a parcel. More mundanely, it may be seen as weaving its colourful pattern into the fabric of our lives. We may be unable to change the motive and with serenity accept it as an overall design, but here and there we may have a chance to choose a different-coloured or textured thread. With courage, we may change what is changeable.

If only we were always wise enough to know which option to take.

2005

142

MRS JONES' MISFORTUNE

or

HOW A LOCAL TORY WARD LOST ONE OF ITS MEMBERS

Mrs Jones' misfortune struck unguardedly in the time it takes to open one's mouth wide to accommodate a new, buttered potato. Just as the smallest of human error or oversight, a wrong word spoken, or too hasty an action taken at a decisive moment in time may bring about a person's downfall or social nemesis, so it took mere seconds to make Mrs Jones the laughing stock of the community.

Mrs Jones, an elderly widow of comfortable means and cherished conservative values, which had made her a staunch supporter of the Tory party, was one day the proud owner of a new pair of dentures. There was nothing to distinguish her acquisition from the false teeth of other senior citizens, except their pristine, blinding whiteness. What a change they made to her life. No one had ever seen such a splendid display of ultra-white, except when Arnold Schwarzenegger smiles at prospective voters or Simon Cowell bares his teeth on X Factor nights.

Although the residents of her mainly Labour-orientated neighbourhood had never quite warmed to her middle England image, they now felt drawn to the array of her new prosthesis as to a magnet. They would engage her in a friendly chat, watching with silent, ill-contained bemusement the object of their mirth, before chuckling, or spluttering with laughter once they were out of earshot.

One day the whiter-than-white spectacle was over. Outside Mrs Jones' bungalow a 'For Sale' sign was erected, and the good lady was now seldom seen to venture abroad. Whenever a neighbour rang the bell - whether out of curiosity or solicitude - she would open the door only as wide as the chain would allow, to utter a few tight-lipped words, while the caller desperately tried to avoid eye contact with her 'impediment'.

One day Mrs Jones was gone, leaving behind for her neighbours and party friends nothing but the story of her misfortune. This would survive for years to come, and whenever lustily recounted, give rise to hearty belly laughs. Allegedly, at least one woman had wet her pants on hearing the story, one octogenarian had suffered a mild heart attack, and several couples would admit that they had laughed all the way to bed that night.

It happened during a fund-raising luncheon of the local Conservative Party, to which Mrs Jones, as a member and faithful supporter, had been invited. Freshly coiffeured, dressed in a blue cashmere twin set and wearing a string of pearls, which she saw as befitting her status in society and the Party, she came to sit opposite a distinguished member of the Ward, who was said to have friends in Central Office and even the Shadow Cabinet.

The plastic chairs of the church hall lacked upholstered comfort, the food was no better or worse than the offering at similar fund-raising events, while due to the extreme narrow width of the tables, people seated opposite each other had between them all but the space of a confessional.

As was her custom nowadays, Mrs Jones flashed her white smiles around, and most keenly at her vis-à-vis, with whom she was soon engaged in an animated conversation. At one stage, fielding her way through a ham salad, she tried to deliver a buttered new potato into her mouth, when - perhaps opening it a little too wide - her wobbly lower denture went AWOL. Catapulting out of her mouth as if released from pressure, it came to rest on a mayonnaise-covered lettuce leaf on the plate of the eminent member opposite.

Briefly, the gentleman looked like someone choking on a fish bone, before he put his knife and fork down in a position which indicated that he had finished his meal. Pointedly, he turned towards the diner on his left, adding a forceful comment on some electoral matter under discussion. This gave the crimson-faced Mrs Jones time to retrieve the fugitive, wrap it in a paper napkin and place it in her bag. Good manners dictated that no one who had witnessed the incident queried the reason for her sudden departure. Looking neither left nor right, her head bowed like a penitent, the good lady stole out of the hall. Yet long after she had gone and the diners had arrived at the mint-and-coffee stage, the esteemed member's misfortune still evoked the odd smile and whispered words of commiseration.

The story of Mrs Jones' misadventure would survive for years to come. Having quickly spread throughout the community, and being suitably embellished by each narrator, it never failed to spice up conversation at the local pub and the table of party hostesses. Finally, it came as no surprise when young children composed a ditty about a denture that had taken to flight.

All the while, local dentists were rubbing their hands: for suddenly people became inordinately concerned for the state of their teeth and some dentures in particular.

No one ever found out where the star of this story had moved to, and whether - having taken her little rascal to a dentist for a tighter fit - she had once again become a pillar of the local Conservative Party in her new place of residence.

2006

OF DREAM FLIGHTS AND SUNFLOWERS

Sometimes I wake up in the middle of the night, unable to go back to sleep. I may then watch late night television, read or do a crossword puzzle. If such activities do not inveigle my mind to switch off due to overload, I turn off the light and shift my thoughts to zero position. Yet although I am seeking sleep like a parched desert traveller an oasis, I remain stuck in the twilight world of the night. Given my mind is not weighed down by anxiety or some unresolved problems, it will gleefully ride back through the layers of the past. As in a dream or on another level of consciousness, places, people and objects will be taking on shape, finally to stand out in amazing detail. While most readily I will return to the happy pastures of early motherhood, or relive experiences which imprinted smiles on me, my mind may also take me back to the rooms that were home for me for the first ten years of my childhood; where I witnessed laughter and play and the gradual awakening to the realities of life, but also the break-up of my parents' marriage. I see the shiny grand piano, on which as a nine year-old I practised Czerny *Études* and my mother played Schubert. I stand in front of the cabinet which housed the gramophone and a collection of His Master's Voice records, among them the Radetzky March, Gigli arias and sultry tango rhythms. My mind returns to the *Kinderzimmer* with its white furniture, teddy bears and a *lanterna magica*; it looks across the roof of a Berliner Hinterhof and crawls into the ship I used to build from an upturned table and a moth-eaten blanket during the hours of lone play. And as if it were yesterday I see our small People's Radio standing high up on my father's bookcase, out of reach of his daughter's hands. Or the kitchen cupboard, on whose shelf my mother used to leave five Reichspfennige every afternoon - the price of the baker's 'Amerikaner' or 'Schnecke'.

The images are clear and mostly in monochrome. Extraordinary, however, is the fact that I quite distinctly remember some nightmares I had as a nine year-old shortly before my parents got divorced, and when their noisy quarrels and my mother's tears were pointing to some imminent far-reaching change in my own life. A feeling of intangible fear and insecurity must have festered in me at the time, for I fell prey to frequent nightmares. A monster, some amorphous dark creature, would be coming up behind me, ready to pounce and devour me. Yet my legs were unable to move, however hard they tried to free themselves from whatever was constraining them. I would wake up, crying, my heart racing, and only my mother's soothing voice would send me back to sleep.

One night I realised that the only way I could escape my nocturnal fiend was by using my arms like wings. And like a bird I raised myself off the ground and high up towards the sky. It remains a mystery to me how my dream-conscious self devised such a rescue, and how in subsequent nightmarish situations I would remember that by using my wing power I was able to escape from an underworld of fear. In recalling such a formula, I can still remember the great sense of freedom that pulsed through me, as I was circling through a cloudless sky like a bird. Indeed, like the seagull Jonathan, whom Richard Bach would later portray so movingly in his classic story for children and adults, and whose flight symbolised physical freedom, while his in-flight thoughts spoke of a human-like wisdom. 'Reading the book gave me wings', said the author Ray Bradbury.

In my nightmares I had a seagull's wings.

2007

When, following my parents' divorce, I came to live in a private children's home, my nightmares ceased. I gradually learned to cope with the loss of my parental home, and with all that such deprivation entails. By proving myself as an outstanding athlete and gymnast, as well as a valuable asset in the school's team sports, I acquired self-esteem. This was followed at an early age by an independence that advocated self-help and trust in the God whom I gradually came to know.

In my fiftieth year, when my marriage broke up, I once again faced survival on my own. Like a derailed train everything that had been driving me in the past had suddenly come to a halt. I seemed to stand on the edge of a bottomless pit, frozen in my loneliness and tempted every morning not to get up and deal with the obstacles around me. One day I discovered that the succour of faith and the catharsis of writing poetry put my life back on its track, while the picture of a sunflower with its radiant face and sturdy stem imparted to me images of Light, Hope and Strength.

Sunflowers, which belong to the *Helianthus* family, are striking summer flowers. Legend will have it that Clytie, a water nymph, was in love with Apollo. But meeting his rejections she died and was changed into a sunflower. Hence she would turn her face to the sun god in his daily course.

Although often painted by children as smiling suns, and popularly believed to turn their heads to the light - a behaviour solely attributed to the genus *Heliotropium* - sunflowers came to symbolise for me an optimistic outlook on life, a philosophy which always searches for the proverbial silver lining or the Miltonian prospect of better days to come.

My mother used to call me a perennial optimist, someone who makes it her business always to look for that bright streak whenever the soul finds itself in the doldrums. Simplistic though it may sound, I may see it in the good tidings that sunflowers convey. For me, the flower's images somehow invite positive thinking and, in a wider sense, are activating my fighting spirit. As such they are my own artless, yet effective way of holding or regaining ground. Perhaps it is not surprising that a framed picture of Jonathan Seagull in full flight, and one a of a smiling sunflower, adorn my walls.

I believe that many of us create our own symbols to boost morale, and to energise the necessary will-power to overcome whatever threatens to blight our lives. And I like to think that God looks kindly on those who attempt to keep up their spirit against all odds, and who in the first instance, and in search of that silver lining or some symbolic rescue hook, will try to help themselves, rather than deposit all their burdens on His shoulders.

2006

THE THIRST FOR KNOWLEDGE

'I find I can have no enjoyment in the world
but the continual drinking of knowledge.'

John Keats

'The desire of knowledge, like the thirst for riches, increases with the acquisition of it', said Laurence Sterne in Tristam Shandy. One may wholeheartedly agree with this notion. I, for one, also believe that the pursuit of knowledge is ultimately why we are here on earth, and why our brains allow us to think rationally in contrast to primates and other animal species.

Although the desire to learn is innate in babies and children, too many men and women in our society often choose mental sloth over the expansion of their mental horizons. Too many never complete their statutory education, nor develop a thirst for the kind of knowledge that will lift them out of the swamp of ignorance, tabloid information and street-wise wisdom. All too often this breed of fellow citizens hand down their lifestyle and mental attitudes to their children, many of whom also remain semi-literate, thus further swelling the ranks of the low-brow, uneducable underclass. What a pity that those unwilling to exercise their brain do not realise what they are missing, and what rewards and power a proper education may bestow. How it may set in motion a continuous learning process that, ultimately, will expand and enrich the personality.

While according to Alexander Pope, 'A little knowledge is a dangerous thing', and while he advocates 'to drink deep or taste not the Pierian spring', because shallow draughts will intoxicate the brain, I believe that even a little learning is better than none, as it will often open the gate to realms of wider cognition. For having once drunk deep from the spring of knowledge, man's thirst for greater erudition will know no limits.

It took me many years to come to that conclusion.

The appetite for learning is like a sweet bug that steals itself into one's system. Yet in some people it never grows, or is killed off in the bud by mundane distractions, illness, an acute fight for survival or a hedonistic lifestyle. In some it will take its course, often frustratingly slow, even reverting to a dormant state at times, while in others it will happily multiply the more knowledge its host acquires.

While wisdom is the sum of individual experiences and knowledge gained over the years, the gathering of knowledge sets its own speed.

For me, it came in leaps and bounds, as did my taste for it.

When I was a child, each day would dawn for me with a host of promises: play after school, perhaps a visit from an aunt, when there would be chocolate éclairs for afternoon coffee; perhaps a walk with my mother in the park, where in autumn I would collect horse chestnuts and spectacularly-tinted leaves, in winter feed birds and red squirrels. I might plan to build a boat from an upturned table and an old blanket after school, pretending to sail the high seas, or a gusty wind might promise a fair flight for my kite. And there were always evenings to look forward to, when my father would challenge me at *Rommé* for one *Reichspfennig* a point. Birthday parties, Easter egg hunting and the wonders of Christmas were further beacons in that still marginalised world of mine.

Learning how to read, write and do arithmetic would later extend my cognitive abilities, but only reading would whet my appetite for knowledge that lay still beyond school and everyday life. Slowly, as I grew older, new wider avenues opened, which begged to be explored.

As a teenager and avid reader of spy and Sherlock Holmes stories, my first career ambition centred on becoming a second Mata Hari or a private detective. German and American films and musicals featuring tap-dancers soon turned my

151

aspirations towards the stage. With two years still to go before leaving school, my father gently persuaded me that, career-wise, I was on the wrong track. However, he allowed me to take tap-dancing lessons, perhaps hoping that with my heavy bone structure, and following my emergence on the national athletics scene as a sprinter and pentathlete, I might lack whatever lissomness or talent was required to make it as a dancer.

He was right, of course. I soon tired of seeing myself as another Marika Röck, the star of German musicals in the early Forties.

It was not long before I focused on a journalistic career. In 1942, six months before sitting my Abitur[1], I decided to apply for a place at the Berlin College of Journalism. My father, who by then was thoroughly disenchanted with National Socialism, made some enquiries and soon presented me with sound arguments why journalistic studies were undesirable in the Reich. Not only would I have to become a member of the Nazi Party, but one of the College's entry requirements was a thorough knowledge of the history of National Socialism and Hitler's rise to power. I would also be expected to quote freely from Hitler's *Mein Kampf*, and convince an interview board that I agreed with the Führer's political and racial policies.

It seemed an awesome task, particularly since I was not interested in politics or the political system. Apart from compulsory Hitler Youth meetings, my spare time was taken up in summer with sporting activities and riding my bike along the Havel river, in winter with ice-skating on the frozen Heiligensee. I had never been given a newspaper to read, and in the private children's home, in which at the age of ten I came to live following my parents' divorce, I only saw the Nazi *Blatt*, the *Völkische Beobachter*, neatly cut up into squares for toilet paper. Furthermore, knowing nothing about

---

[1] Baccaluareate

the art of Nazi reportage and government media censorship, I was surely the least likely candidate for a career in journalism. Yet, stubborn as I was, I came close to joining the Party, before I saw the wisdom of filing away another vocational dream.

Developments on the Russian and Western fronts, and the gruesome impact of Allied air raids over Berlin and other German cities, soon ended any young person's chance of continuing education. Whether school leavers were drafted into war service in rural areas, ammunition factories or anti-flak batteries, career ambitions had to be shelved pending the outcome of the war. All that now mattered was to stay alive, not to perish under bombs or in a phosphorus inferno. Later, at the end of the war, instincts focused on survival. In Russian-occupied territory they also focused on living with rape, or its evasion, by soldiers who had been given *carte blanche* in the treatment of German women.

It was a time when vacancies for work were as scarce as lottery wins, and no social benefits formed a lifeline for the unemployed. I would, therefore, accept any job that was offered, however demanding, humbling or weird, in order to stay on my feet. Experience was thus handed down to me on a plate, as was knowledge of human nature and, revealingly, of myself.

When in the British Zone in 1948 an opportunity arose for German girls to go to England, either to train as nurses or domestics in hospitals, I applied for a cleaner's job at Oxford's Radcliffe Infirmary, in the hope of being able to boost my English with studies at university level.

I passed the English Labour Office's requirements with flying colours: a clean political record, a good working knowledge of English and 'freedom from sexually-transmitted diseases'. The latter was established by a medical examination of the "private parts" of all applicants, which was a most humiliating experience, especially since my knowledge of this scourge was literally non-existent. Most of my fellow applicants were equally immature in 'worldly' matters and professed still to be virgins.

Although in post-war England, where wartime restrictions were only slowly easing up, and I initially faced much hostility as a 'Nazi' or a 'Kraut', life suddenly allowed me to look forward again. The desire to study, to gain new knowledge and to find a career niche into which I might fit, gripped me like a fever.

Henceforth experience did not come in droplets, but in cataract fashion. In Oxford's Radcliffe Hospital, I scrubbed and polished miles of wooden corridor floors on my knees, scoured bathrooms and bowed to the foibles of supervisors and ward sisters, before I was promoted to the dizzy height of Matron's Maid. Off-duty I read novels by Thomas Hardy and Jane Austen and other prescribed literary texts, and studied Shakespeare's sonnets and romantic poetry. Eighteen months after setting foot in England, I passed the University's 'Proficiency in English' (A-level English) exam with an upper grade. And now nothing could stop me on the path to further education.

First I opted for a spell as an assistant psychiatric nurse in a mental hospital. Here the work was extremely stressful. On an 'Acute Ward' one needed to pack one's ears and insulate one's nerves with cotton wool, and at the end of a shift, be able to purge from one's mind the often nightmarish sounds and images that will assail staff in the course of their duty.

I, for one, did not manage this daily mind-cleansing routine. I therefore decided to top up my studies of mental illness with a three-year course in general nursing. Yet on successful completion, and having followed up my training with a stint as a staff nurse at the British Military Hospital in Berlin, I still did not see nursing as my ultimate career. Little was I to know at the time that in later years my nursing and medical knowledge would prove invaluable assets.

Henceforth my life continued on an erratic course, which several times saw me seriously ill or on the operating table. Once again my vision of the future was blocked, my thirst for greater knowledge put on hold.

New vistas opened up again when I got married and gave birth to three sons. Suddenly I had found a career, that of wife and loving mother. It was enough for me at the time. If well done, it was surely a full-time job, I thought, and I was not yet emancipated enough to feel that I had to prove myself in some professional field.

Perhaps this is why I see those years as the happiest of my life.

My marriage ended in 1978, and since my sons were students at Glasgow University, I moved to Scotland. It was a time when unemployment was on the rise, and career ambition often had to bow to financial considerations. Working as a bi-lingual university secretary meant survival for me. It also left me enough time to do undergraduate studies and, in my leisure hours, to listen to my inner voices which cried out to be heard and put on paper.

As part of a cathartic healing process I began writing poetry and short stories, some of which won prizes or were published. And now life was suddenly full of options again, full of challenges which asked not to be ignored.

A literary award for The Naked Years, my first autobiography, was the result of meticulous research and years of writing. Since then every book of mine has borne the stamp of my life's experiences. My writing also echoes sentiments, the pain of suffering and loneliness, while often enough it is jubilant with the joy of living. An attentive reader might also detect my continuing greed to widen my boundaries of perception.

Thus late in life, and often via a circuitous route, creative writing became more than a hobby. It became a beloved occupation, if not an inner urge.

Now that I am well into my Eighth Age, and on more than one occasion have had to face my mortality, my thirst for knowledge still knows no bounds. So little time left, my grey cells seem to declare, so much still to learn, to experience, to think through. Writing, and seeking greater knowledge, has turned into a life force which sustains me - a Faustian ambition, to learn *was die Welt zusammenhält*, what holds the world together.

At the age of eighty, my uncle began to study Arabic; an aunt of mine made a name for herself as a painter in watercolours when she was well into her seventies. Another relative wrote a clever book on Nietzsche and built up a family archive when he retired from medical practice. No limits are seemingly set in old age to extend one's frontiers of knowledge, or develop dormant skills. It is surely a formula which makes the remaining years of life mentally exciting and rewarding, thus keeping the rut out of the daily routine. Perhaps it is also a secret of longevity, and how the elderly may remain a reckonable, exploitable source of wisdom for the younger generation.

I don't know what inspires me to search for answers in the realms of metaphysics or why I like esoteric subjects. I don't know what makes me want to learn about the exploration of the Universe, the origin and evolution of mankind, and the final frontiers. Or about aspects of religion and the forces of Good and Evil. Perhaps there is a deeper sense in it all: a search for God and the purpose of our life here on earth.

As a writer, history has lately begun to fascinate me, too; so do the changes in our society. Yet studies in these subjects also increase sorrow for the state of mankind. They impart knowledge that does not enrich the soul.

There are also many things that I should still like to do or see before I reach The Bar, to speak with Tennyson. So much that still abides. Yet much of it does no longer lie within my physical powers or bows out to common sense. As for most of

156

us who are of an advanced age, such realisation does not come easy. Yet we have to accept our physical limitations and whatever forms a barrier to the fulfilment of seasoned dreams. It is an acceptance, I believe, that grows not so much out of the inevitable but the wisdom of age. It is empirical in nature, reinforced by rational thinking.

As for me, I shall thus not make it to the Taj Mahal before my time is up, nor to the Tibetan foothills; neither shall I be snorkelling on the Barrier Reef or driving down the Pacific Highway. I shall never swim again in the Red Sea, with the sun setting behind the Sahara Desert, nor watch the dawn from the peak of Hong Kong's Lantao Island. And only in my mind can I ski downhill over virgin snow or bathe in a serene, unpolluted lake...

But then there remains still so much to do, and so much to learn. It would seem that I have no time to feel old. My thirst for more knowledge will act both as an elixir and an impelling force.

2007

A TIME TO BE BORN, A TIME TO DIE

'I have no time', we often say. But what is Time? Nobody has yet been able to analyse 'absolute Time', which dictionaries define as the continuous existence of a sequence which we divide into periods. I suppose nobody ever will.

Our awareness of Time regulates our daily activities; it fixes calendar events and creates past and future perspectives. It also gives us a concept of history, allows scientists to determine the stages of evolution and even the approximate age of our globe and universe. Time for us sets its own pace. It may race like a Grand National horse, amble, canter or slog along like a pack-horse, but it will never stop for a breather. Yet a new, highly sophisticated and controversial theory, developed by Julian Barber, a British physicist, would like us to believe now that there may be no Time at all, and that all cycles are only part of a greater 'timeless rotation'. He admits, and many scientists agree, that Time is 'a troublesome entity to physicists, a real problem at the heart of science'. He suggests that 'Time' is an illusion, not a fundamental concept. His frustratingly technical theory will have most of us staring at a solid wall. What, we may ask ourselves, if the universe had no beginning and no end? What if there is no real past or future? Meanwhile, all we - who are unable to follow Barnes' conjecture - can do is to continue living with Time. For we live by the clock, we plan our days by the calendar, and our bodies are attuned to a biological rhythm interconnected with Time. Without our perception of it we would surely float through life like astronauts in their capsule. And what would happen to the process of growth? How would day and night fit into a 'timeless' world, and how the changing seasons which, like the ageing process, are the basic road markers of Time? But then, there are so many things beyond human understanding, so many things that scientists are still trying to unravel...

158

It is a simple and acknowledged fact that the older we grow the faster we think time is passing. The weeks, the days, the hours seem to shrink. 'My God, how time flies', we cry, seeing Time as an enemy, as the winged chariot that hurries near us. Yet, that time will stop for us for good one day is a fact which we have to address and accept. Some of us may dwell on our final exit in morbid fashion, others will bow to their ultimate fate and channel remaining energies into well-spent time. For them, Time has become a treasured commodity.

In the OT Book of Ecclesiastes the 'Philosopher' declares that 'There is a time to be born, and a time to die'. What sounds so elementary in its essence is in its philosophy still far removed from the understanding of young people. Not before middle age, or when faced with a serious illness, do most of us become aware of our mortality. Often we do so with a shock. We may experience a *Torschlusspanik*, an eleventh-hour mentality. So little time left, we groan, so much we are still hoping to achieve. And with an ache in our hearts we realise that Time is incorruptible, that it makes no concessions, nor trades in an expanded life span for a soul. Once we reach Shakespeare's Seventh Age, or our century's Eighth, we have no choice but to confront dying and death head-on.

For many among us it is the inevitability of death which finally makes us resigned to what the 'Philosopher' sees as the 'eternal circle'. It is then only a question of finding a formula as to how to give our remaining years optimum quality.

Some elderly people manage to do this on a grand scale - travel, a change of lifestyle, a new hobby. They may take up painting, study a foreign language, work for a charity, try their hand at collages or write a book. Subject to physical ability and mental agility, no limits are seemingly set to such endeavours. For others, for whom such options are not, or are no longer available, each day may offer less challenging, but no less quantitative rewards: a good read, listening to music, entertaining friends, visiting family or pursuing interests that lie within one's scope. And how many pensioners will sing the praise of their garden, allotment or greenhouse, in which their declining years still allow them to potter around in unison with Nature? The list of activities and indulgences which will take the sting out of the thought of dying is long.

Let us, who are of an advanced age, be grateful then, if we are still able to laugh and play and reap what in hard work and with loving care we have sown during our earlier years. Let us celebrate the cameo joys of life as long as we can. And having made peace with our dust-to-dust existence, let us nourish the hope that in the end we shall not face the Marvellian 'deserts of vast eternity', but that we shall be welcomed by a Loving, Shining Light, and by whatever eternal life the Scriptures are promising those of faith.

SHARED REVISION

We are doing Biology today. That is, revision for my daughter's Baccalaureate exam. Yesterday it was English literature. My God, it made me feel backward. Couldn't remember the name of the main character in Kafka's novel, the one who changed into a beetle overnight. My memory was equally fuzzy when, just for starters, we analysed the mysticism in A Midsummer Night's Dream. If only I had paid more attention to Mrs Golightly, my English teacher. But then all I had in mind at the time were girls. Now, willingly coerced by parental love and duty, I have become a mature student at the kitchen table. I admit that I often feel like I am being stranded on *terra incognita*. And I wonder, whether my frequent non-knowledge will shake my daughter's respect for her father's IQ. You see, suddenly I am no longer the child's all-knowing Dad, no longer the teenager's encyclopaedia.

As I said, we're doing biology today, a subject which nowadays commands an awesome latitude. So far we've dealt with morphogenesis, homeostasis and the process of photosynthesis. Believe me, I'm making a great effort to brush up or assimilate new knowledge, even if such enlightenment doesn't wash the dishes or raise my status at work.

My daughter, bless her, is doing fine. She's convinced that with me by her side, asking questions and checking answers, and with her tutoring me in return, our shared revision augurs well for an upper grade. Meanwhile, my own singleness of mind is bound to flatter her. It even makes her ignore her mobile, her music and that skimpy thing in some shop window, which she had earlier said she simply must have.

Life has certainly changed these past few days. We live on sandwiches, baked beans, pizzas and whatever the wife left in the freezer before she went visiting her mother. Mind you, the kitchen and bathroom are in a bit of a mess, and the weeds in the garden are celebrating their halcyon days. But then our work has priority. As long as daughter will do well in her exams, my refresher course will have been worth the mental slog.

Tomorrow we're doing French. Oh, *Mon Dieu*!

ANGELS

Let me state to begin with: I believe in angels. Mind you, not in the conventional image of heavenly beings with feathered wings, nor in droll, rosy-cheeked cherub types, but in administering divine spirits often referred to as guardian angels.

While we cannot see angels in their true form, most of us who believe in them will feel comfortable with their definition as a spiritual force that flows through the universe, protecting and guiding us, if and when this is so divined: a power that exudes love and compassion, and often directs us, by speaking through our inner voice. This agency has never let me down - not since I learnt to listen to it.

In trying to prove the existence of angels, we are bound to come up against a wall; for we would have to explore the realm where the spirit and science meet, and which is often cited as the space in which there hover things beyond man's cognition.

It is interesting to note that all cultures acknowledge the existence of angels or celestial spirits, and how over the centuries popular conception of them has changed. In Jewish, Christian and Muslim belief, angels are supernatural beings, intermediaries between God and humans. Martin Luther described angels as 'spiritual beings created by God without a body for the service of Christendom and the Church'. Voltaire said in his Philosophical Dictionary that it is not known where angels dwell - whether in the air, the Great Void or on the planets, and that 'it has not been God's pleasure that we should be informed about their abode'. To Christians they represent everything that is good, benevolent, graceful and pure at heart. Mohammedans see them as genii who were created from pure bright gems. In the fifth century AD, Dionysius divided them into nine orders, while the Bible lists seven holy angels. In his writings, Thomas Aquinas, the famous theologian and philosopher of the Middle Ages (also known as the Angelic Doctor because of the excellence and purity of his teachings), discussed the existence and nature of angels, while as early as the second century certain heretics were known to have advocated the worship of angels. Modern scientists, on the other hand, now define angels as photons and elementary particles of light, as some ethereal manifestation which, arguably, have no proven divine purpose or effectiveness.

Ever since - according to the Gospel - an Angel of the Lord appeared to Joseph in his dream, to Mary in the Annunciation and, in the company of other heavenly beings, to the shepherds at Bethlehem, angels have featured strongly in Western art. Many Gothic and Renaissance painters, sculptors, cathedral stone masons and book illustrators have created them as corporeal beings with wings. One of their earliest representations in our culture dates from AD 1015, the high-relief detail from a bronze door of the Hildesheim Minster. Angels have been depicted on friezes, church ceilings and triptychs, in paintings, and as winged cherubs in fine plaster and bronze work. Lithographers, such as Gustave Doré, embellished the Bible and major works by Dante, Rabelais, Cervantes and Poe with such heavenly entities.

In Victorian times, angels figured most prominently. The winged variety even sat on gravestones and were frequently the motif for artwork. During my early schooldays, we collected and exchanged pictures of cherubs as adults did cigarette coupons, and whatever youngsters may fancy collecting today.

Angels are of course more accessible, more seemingly tangible, in physical form. Once the feather-winged kind had been created by man's imagination, the writers and illustrators of children's fiction thrived on them, just as the Church still does in its preachings. They also figure in hymns and biblical texts as messengers bringing good tidings and speaking in heavenly tongues.

In our age - apart from the odd account of some 'presence' - angels seem to have outlived their winged, corporeal image; they are also passé in modern paintings. No one I questioned, and who believed in guardian angels, visualised them in physical form, and angels seem to have all but disappeared from modern children's fiction. Many people say they do not believe in them, adding that they are 'not into religion'. Yet, interestingly, some confirmed agnostics see them as a benevolent spiritual force, albeit an unfathomable one.

Whether this force is called 'guardian angel' or the 'Holy Spirit', the mystery of angels will continue to have a place among the false idols of our society, in which science and cosmology are conquering an ever wider space.

Throughout the centuries, there have been alleged sightings of angels. In Britain alone, eight hundred accounts of people who claim to have been visited by them were gathered by PhD student Emma Heathcote for an Everyman TV programme in December 2000. Her findings also confirmed that there has been an upsurge in the number of people reported to have witnessed a manifestation.

Apart from stories of visitations recounted by individuals, one group experience stands out. This was reluctantly revealed by the Rector of a Hertfordshire village church not so long ago as having been shared by the churchwarden, the organist and a thirty-strong congregation. Apparently, during the baptism of a twenty year-old woman, people suddenly saw a male-like figure in a near-transparent white robe standing near the font. It had no wings, nor a beard, but no one was in any doubt that it was an angel. The apparition lasted only a few seconds, during which time seemed to stand still. No words were spoken, and people would afterwards admit to having been gripped by a warm sensation, and to the church being suffused by a scent reminiscent of rose petals.

It was remarkable that subsequently the witnesses closed ranks, declining to talk publicly about their 'privileged' experience. All would maintain that God had spoken to them and that their lives had changed significantly since. Only when giving evidence for the Everyman programme - on condition that their church remain unidentified - did they agree to speak freely about the unheralded visitation.

I for one have much reason to believe that an angel, in the form of a divine 'helper', is watching over me and guiding me, and I find the existence of such a force comforting. According to John Polkinghorne in God In An Age of Science, that force or spirit may indeed have a divine participation. Yet it is surely bound forever to remain unquantifiable and unproven, notwithstanding the fact that Professor Hawking, the eminent wheelchair-bound physicist, sees physics as a challenge to produce an explanation of Everything. While, according to Hawking, mankind will become extinct in 1,000 years due to global warming or a planetary accident, I doubt that even by then, in what is a mere flash in human time, the existence of angels will have been proven, and their 'dwelling place' discovered, by even the most complex mathematical equations and quantum theories.

So, until we reach the heavenly gate, let us believe in them as in something that is good and pure and beautiful, and which resides in that uncomputable empyrean space.

Let us also acknowledge, and praise, the men and women in our midst, who, shunning the limelight, live their lives like angels - devoid of self-interest and magnanimous in caring for others; people who with their saint-like actions, which do not ask for medals, form an antidote to many ills of this world - human angels who are drawing strength and goodness from their faith and a deep bourne of love.

2006

TRAVELLING WITH MY HERMÈS

You want to fly to Paris or Berlin? Perhaps to New York, Hong Kong or some place which many of us would have to try and find on a map? No problem. The computer will do it all for you. No hassle, no headache trying to calculate the time difference. All you have to do is to present yourself at the airport on time. And experienced traveller that you are, you will have duly checked your ticket. You will also have worked out how much time you'll need to get to the airport for the required check-in procedure, planning in a possible tailback on the M25, a slow-moving farm vehicle on a rural road, train delays due to wet leaves on the line, or to some alcohol-sodden motorist having come to serious harm on an unguarded level crossing. You will also know that - apart from a few sterling and foreign notes - your credit card and travellers' cheques are your safest financial companions abroad. One might say that you have become quite blasé by now as regards the necessary travel arrangements. Well, good for you. Have a good flight.

Twenty-five years ago booking a flight to anywhere outside Europe would have required the expertise of a travel agent as well as one's own careful pre-flight checks. And never more so than if one were a single woman inexperienced in the art of booking a long-haul flight.

During the years of my marriage, and up to the late Seventies, all continental and Far Eastern flights for my ex-pat family had been processed by the Ministry of Defence, my husband's employer. My husband would merely make sure that we left in good time for the airport check-in, keeping in mind road and weather conditions, the possibility of a broken shoe-lace or whatever has the unholy habit of demanding last-minute attention.

So how did I, by now a single, middle-aged woman, get to Boston, Massachusetts, USA, one day in the Eighties? The very thought of that venture still makes adrenaline seep into my system. But then, the fact that I made it at all had surely been the luck of a first-time trans-Atlantic traveller.

I was living in Scotland at the time, when I received an invitation from the American and British International Biographical Institutes to attend their World Congress in Boston and give a talk on How To Write An Autobiography. Such honour had apparently been conferred on me on the strength of my first book The Naked Years, which surprisingly had made a great impact in America.

I accepted and immediately earmarked the venue on my atlas. I checked my wardrobe, deciding to treat myself to a smart suit, so that I would make a fine 'English' figure at the lectern. In order to make quite sure that I got a flight that would take me to Boston before 4 pm on the day of Congress Registration, I went straight to a travel agent.

'Make sure', I said to the young woman who constantly fiddled with her blonde tresses, 'that I get there on time. The time difference...' With child-like trust in 'Blondie's' computations, I left it to her to find a suitable flight. So far, so good. But that is how many horror stories begin.

In the weeks that followed, I worked on my lecture, updated my wardrobe and bought some travellers' cheques. Although I would incur no charges for the hotel room or any meals and excursions, I looked forward to strolling, one session-free afternoon, through the city's shopping streets to buy something genuinely Bostonian or American.

However, I never thought of checking my flight details. My trust in a travel agent's know-how was still unshakeable.

Two days prior to departure I packed my suitcase. I always like to do this at leisure, without time breathing down my neck. My smart Hermès 'special occasion' and travel handbag, recklessly acquired in a recent designer sale, contained my passport, flight ticket, a roll of peppermints, fifty US dollars and fifty pounds sterling. All that I would have to do would be to transfer the contents of my day-to-day bag to my posh one.

The morning before I was due to set out on my maiden visit to America, I decided to do some gardening. I dead-headed, and watered the roses, and weeded flower beds with gusto. At 11 am - the time factor plays an important role in my story - I went indoors for a cup of coffee, and in order to phone the airport for confirmation of next day's flight.

The voice on the phone exploded in disbelief. 'But madam, your flight is leaving in 25 minutes!'

Lightning could not have struck me more forcefully. 'What?' I cried, feeling poisonous snakes wriggling in the pit of my stomach. I realised it would take at least twenty minutes to get to the airport. 'Please, hold the flight?' I pleaded, 'I'll try and make it.'

The voice, by now impassioned, and with a soupçon of arrogance reserved for passengers from the backwoods, replied in the negative. I banged down the receiver, took a deep breath and allowed rational thinking to take over. I called a local taxi and explained my situation, staccato, my mind computing the chances of still making the flight.

'I'll be with you in two minutes', replied the driver.

There I was. Dressed in my gardening clothes, my hands soiled, my nails waiting to be manicured, my hair to be shampooed. I congratulated myself on having packed and locked my suitcase earlier. By the time the taxi arrived, I had secured the house and paid the bathroom a flying visit. The driver grabbed my suitcase, I grabbed my smart bag and off we were as for a speed trial.

'Can't tell whether we'll make it', said the driver, 'all depends on the traffic.' He phoned the airline, explained, gave his location on the motorway and estimated time of arrival, all the while driving as if pursued by a police car.

For the first time I had a good look at myself. I thought of my smart new suit still hanging in the wardrobe; I winced at my clothes, my soil-ringed fingernails. I felt naked without any make-up. And my shoes! Uncharitable thoughts went through my head, condemning 'Blondie' to everlasting penance. But then again, should I not have checked the ticket? Alright, so it was *mea culpa*.

At the airport terminal the driver stopped, tyres squealing, like a racing driver coming to the pit for a tyre change. He sprinted to the check-in desk, which was about to close. Not taking 'No' for an answer, he heaved my luggage onto the scales. 'I phoned earlier on behalf of my passenger', he told the check-in staff. No muscle stirred in the woman's face. She phoned, explained, argued, turned towards me. 'They are about to close the door of the aircraft', she said, 'but try, if you will. Did you pack your suitcase yourself? Have you got any inflammables in it? Any...?'

My legs were dancing on the spot.

At last, the boarding card. My taxi driver, bless his soul, got hold of a nearby trolley, told me to stand on it and 'drove' at speed to Customs. I had only time to air my thanks, before I was whisked onwards to the aircraft as on a conveyor belt. One stewardess shoved me into the cabin, another had her hand on whatever button or switch closes aircraft doors. Immediately the plane started moving. I had made it.

All eyes were upon me, the last passenger, the woman who carried a beautiful designer handbag, yet who wore clothes that should surely have gone to an Oxfam shop. And what about her hair? That stain on her trousers? And just look at that T-shirt...

I was shown to the only economy seat left. A partition wall in front of my seat threatened limited leg space. Half of my seat was taken up by the blubber-like arm of a seriously obese woman, a mother with a baby in a cot. Predictably, the little brute began to exercise its lungs as soon as the flight took off and the aircraft gained altitude. However, its mother was too absorbed in what I took to be a Mills & Boon novel to take any notice. Well, I thought, I had made it, but at what a price. I settled into my half of the seat, dreading the torture ahead.

We had not long been in the air when I noticed that I had forgotten to transfer the contents of my day-to-day handbag to my Hermès traveller. I was on the way to America without a cheque book, travellers' cheques, bank card, diary and whatever paraphernalia women like to carry around with them. The implications did not bear thinking about. Close to tears, I clutched my Hermès like a teddy bear.

At some point during the flight, I noticed that in the heat of my departure, I had also forgotten to take my watch. I asked a stewardess what time and day it was, and that was when the real fun started: when I realised that 'Blondie' had messed up the flight dates, and that I would be arriving in Boston, and in my hotel, one day too early. Now all that I had left was to utter a silent, unladylike expletive.

Needless to say I did not get any sleep during the flight, pumped up as I was with adrenaline. Perhaps I ought to have forcibly claimed my whole seat space, perhaps objected to the olfactory affront of a seriously soiled nappy.

Boston. A miracle: my suitcase had made it despite my hell-bent check-in. A taxi, its driver a swarthy individual, the kind I would not like to meet in a dark alley at night, and certainly not engage in a fare dispute, least of all dare to question the choice of route. It soon became clear to me that the driver did not take a direct route to the hotel. He would turn into every side street, negotiated one roundabout twice, and once declared the need for making a 'slight' detour due to some alleged road-works further ahead.

'You'd better try and make the hotel soon', I said. 'I haven't got many dollars on me.'

'How many have you got?'

'Fifty', the fool in me admitted.

'That'll do.'

In less than a minute the car pulled up at the 5-star hotel and I parted with my fifty dollars.

When I asked for a room for the night, the receptionist eyed me with overt suspicion. No wonder. My appearance would not have met the *niveau* of her classy hotel.

'I'm afraid', I began, explaining my situation which - let's face it - sounded rather improbable, even fictitious. I thought she was weighing up the odds in her mind when her eyes fell on my Hermès bag, admiring, envious, desirous, and accepting the ownership of such an item as my credentials.

'I need a fifty dollar deposit', she said. 'Hotel policy.'

'I have none left', I admitted, 'the taxi driver charged me all that I had on me.'

'What?' Incredulity spread on the woman's face. 'You should not have paid more than ten dollars. It's only a 5-minute ride from the airport. Have you got some sterling?'

I counted out £35, all that remained after having paid my Samaritan on wheels back home.

'Can you phone your bank?'

'English banks are closed on Sundays. Anyway, I haven't got the telephone number. My diary…'

The sentinel behind the counter took my sterling notes, gave me a room key, called the porter, smiled.

The room did not deny its 5-star status. A similar one in England would have cost me a week's salary. I inspected the state-of-the-art bathroom, made myself a cup of tea and, in the absence of food - or money to pay for it - I liberally laced it with cream and sugar. There came a knock at the door.

'I thought you might be hungry', said the young woman in hotel uniform. Her chiselled English suggested a privileged upbringing and an elite girls' school. 'I heard about your misfortune.' She put down a tray of sandwiches, a glass of milk and fruit. 'Perhaps you can ask your Conference Directors for some money tomorrow.'

My stomach called her an angel in disguise.

I had a bath, shampooed my hair, had a change of clothes. That evening I ordered dinner in the restaurant and had it charged to my room. My world was - at least to some extent - back in order.

Well, I was lent some dollars, my lecture went down well, and on the day of departure I got a taxi driver who charged me $8.50 for the 5-minute drive to the airport.

All that happened many years ago. I have since become a seasoned traveller. I book online, being perfectly able to compute the time difference on continental and intercontinental journeys. And in case you ask, my Hermès bag is still travelling with me, still design-proud, its leather shining.

2009

TAKING PART WAS WHAT COUNTED

The low regard in which physical education is still held in most state schools has often been highlighted by the media, since in our computer-orientated society the merits of fresh air, competitive spirit and fair play lost out to educational reforms. School sports became the Cinderella of the National Curriculum.

Decades ago, modern track and field events were still fostered in schools, as was the sporting ethos. Instead of producing - among other notable sportsmen - athletes of the Roger Black and Steve Cram mould, the decline of mind- and body-building school sports has made many youngsters find other outlets for their energy. They are seen hanging about, bored, mindlessly kicking a ball around or engaging in activities that bear the hallmark of street culture. Such 'pastimes' do not require a special effort, no character-boosting expansion of physical and mental stamina. Yet these are the virtues, which, acquired in early years, will stand young people in good stead once they enter our competitive society.

Now and then, urgent calls can be heard by politicians and teachers for putting athletics and games back on the curriculum. It remains to be seen whether this is wishful thinking or whether regular PT in the affected schools will experience a renaissance.

In Germany, Hitler's rise to power in 1933 brought a revolution to the school curriculum. Instead of religious studies, a daily PT period was introduced, as was a weekly games afternoon. We soon came to be at home in the gym and on the sports field, as physical training became a major subject at school. The motive for the implementation of a rigorous sports programme was obvious: Hitler wanted a strong, healthy and resilient youth. What was not immediately evident was that this served his own political purpose.

174

Yet it was the concept of *Körperliche Ertüchtigung* which aimed at physical fitness, that enabled us to fight for survival in the years to come. It certainly made me fit. It also kindled in me an interest in athletics.

In my day athletics, like any other competitive sports disciplines, was a true amateur pastime. No appearance or prize money provided incentives. A competitive spirit was needed, a drive to win, but no less an understanding that taking part was what counted. Perhaps it brought out the best in each competitor. Winners would enjoy the brief limelight of success, perhaps a mention in the sports column of the *Völkische Beobachter*, or their local 'blatt'.

Young athletes would participate in local Games, and if they were promising material, in championships at national level. In larger cities the over-eighteens might join an athletics club and have facilities for training. However, younger boys and girls with good running speeds or an aptitude for field events were managed by the Hitler Youth, which treated such youngsters like prize race-horses whose wins would serve the political profile of the organisation.

I had the doubtful, yet enjoyable privilege of belonging to that cosseted group of young athletes. For me, this entailed a much-valued fringe benefit. By blaming my frequent absence at Hitler Youth cadre meetings and rallies on my training commitment, I did not incur official censure, nor did my 'truancy' lead to more serious repercussions. Indeed, such leniency suggested that the local Hitler Youth gurus saw me as a valuable pawn in the Nazi promotion of 'Strength Through Sport'. What they did not realise was that I all too often preferred a cycle ride, a swim or an afternoon at the cinema to serious training.

The early Forties were my athletic heyday, before malnutrition, and lack of sleep due to the nightly air strikes on neighbouring Berlin, sapped my energy, and disaffection with a politically-run sport deflated my enthusiasm as a sprinter and pentathlete. What I remember of it today is my ambition to excel in sport. Games and championships also provided a welcome change from my love-deprived environment, while fighting for every centimetre and tenth of a second strengthened my mental and physical backbone. It was certainly a handsome fillip.

In those days, my generation still embraced an artless national patriotism, the kind of loyalty which - apart from today's football culture - seems to have faded or totally disappeared from our self-centred, globally oriented society. In the late Thirties and Forties, young, talented German athletes were expected to compete 'for the glory of the movement and the country'. And Hitler's 'Pride of the Nation' obliged, and quite willingly, for it was an honour to be picked. Not that one could choose, fancying one event more than another. One was told when and in which discipline one was to participate. But then, what fun it was, to find oneself on a stage for a day or two, being cheered on by the spectators. And what bliss to win and enjoy star status. After all, they say, a little pride sits becomingly on a champion. Indeed, which young athlete would not have enjoyed the panegyrics of a journalist who compared my first impact on the under-eighteen sports scene with a Caesarian quotation: *'Veni, vidi, vici'* - 'I came, I saw, I conquered'. Or who would not feel flattered on reading in the local edition of the *Völkische Beobachter* that all boys and girls from Potsdam and the Land Brandenburg were 'keeping their fingers crossed' that I would do well at the European Youth Championships in Milan, 'for the honour and the glory of German youth'?

Our dress was simple: loose-fitting black shorts, held together at the waist and thighs with elastic, and a white vest emblazoned with the Hitler Youth emblem. Prizes for the winners in each discipline were certificates or novels promoting either National Socialist doctrines on German woman- and manhood, or celebrating German-ness with all its associated notions - books which, I am sure, were seldom read. I do not remember what happened to my book trophies. Did I throw them away or did they end up on some bottom shelf? I think I had a sixth sense for what promised to be a boring read. By then I was devouring books by Galsworthy, Kipling and Warwick Deeping in translation, which conveyed a fascinating world to me. And what passionate emotions did I encounter in Tolstoy's Anna Karenina, the novel which I found on my grandmother's bookshelf, and which I had to read in secret, as my mother deemed it unsuitable for a sixteen year-old.

Book prizes and certificates were accompanied by a handshake from a prominent Hitler Youth leader and a Heil Hitler salute. In the autumn of 1931 I did even better at the European Youth Championships in Milan (*La Campionati Sportivi della Giuventis Europea*). As a member of the German 4 x 100 m relay team, I received a silver cup from the then Italian Minister for Foreign Affairs, Count Ciano. (I regret to this day that in 1945, shortly before the take-over of the Tangermünde by American troops, I buried the cup in the garden in the belief that a potential enemy interrogator might not look too kindly on such an acquisition.)

The eyes of Hitler Youth leaders seemed to be constantly upon me. When I was fifteen, and my breasts began to swell, a *Gruppenführerin* approached me after a successful 100 m sprint. Through the din of cheers from Hitler Youth boys and girls, the stern-looking official told me that it was time I was wearing a bra. 'Your... eh...can be seen bobbing under your vest', she said, pointing to my poking nipples. 'This is causing comments among the boys, you know.' Needless to say, I had to acquire what in those days young girls equated with a contraption.

My training after school was not organised and often quite perfunctory. For in the days of hard rationing my diet invariably consisted of fried potatoes, skimmed milk puddings and thin soup enriched with the odd piece of gristle, a pitiable fare on which to build a top performance on the track and in the field events. But like my fellow athletes I would just give my best. Like them I ran, jumped, hurdled, threw the javelin and putted the shot because I was bitten by the competitive bug, and because I had come to realise that will-power and a fighting spirit were good companions in life.

Their seeds were sown, I believe, at the 1936 Olympic Games in Berlin, when my father and I watched two weeks of athletics from a terrace seat. In 'The Naked Years', I recalled the sentiments of the barely eleven year-old at the sight of sport at its best; as I shared the tension of the competitors, the champions' euphoria, the losers' disappointment and the spectators' excitement. I saw Jesse Owens setting new world records, and the Finnish runners triumphing over the long distances; I clenched my teeth every time a high-jump or pole-vault favourite attempted a new height. I bit my nails, cheered, applauded or sighed in chorus with the crowd.

The athletes' fighting spirit impressed me most, their battle to gain the edge over their fellow competitors, for which they had to tap their last physical reserves. Perhaps it was their motivation, their singleness of mind, which left a legacy in me.

Apart from the kudos of participating in the Olympic Games, competitive athletics is now a multimillion pound business and an entertainment industry. Large sums of money are paid out to winners, and attendance money ensures that promoters do not end up with a deficit. In the United States, bonuses are allegedly pledged to athletes, if they break existing records. Indeed, fortunes can be made by those who cleverly bank their prowess. Top-billed athletes are cosseted by clubs and athletic associations, but few would seem to compete solely for the honour of taking part. Athletics has become a business and, by dint of extensive media coverage, for many a Vanity Fair. Increasingly, we hear, it also becomes a parody of the sport, in that star athletes change their country and their allegiances in what is described as a growing trade. Immoral and unethical as it may be, the fact remains that many athletes are for sale. Siphoned off by wealthier countries, they change their nationality like a vest and use the country's emblem like a flag of convenience. They are the sport's mercenaries, a saleable product, and athletics is poorer for it.

Other blots on today's athletics landscape are surely anabolic steroids and other performance-enhancing drugs with which cheats will try and boost their winning chances. Such substances were unknown or unobtainable in my day, as was the range of fitness training without which no self-respecting athlete would nowadays enter the arena. Which athlete in bygone days would have wanted to, or been able to afford, the ostentatious gold chains now worn by many sprinters around their necks? I wonder whether such adornment is to emphasise the wearer's financial status in the world of sport, just as an expensive car has long been the show-off object of a man's wealth and social standing.

While nobody would deny a top athlete the pride of achievement, some champions score low on the humility scale. The swagger they adopt once applause is spreading a red carpet for them, and the arrogance some exude when facing lesser mortals, seem to proclaim 'I'm the greatest', the kind of imperious self-evaluation reminiscent of a certain world-champion boxer.

In my day there were no Africans or black Americans to compete against, and it must have been quite a shock to Hitler's Germanic *Weltanschauung* to see Jesse Owens winning four gold medals at the Berlin Olympics. Much was later made of the fact that Hitler left the stadium before the medal ceremony, claiming some urgent business of state, a *faux pas* later popularly attributed to his refusal to shake the hand of the black athlete. Be that as it may, I do not remember any public outcry against Jesse Owens, the 'nigger', the common, often naïve description in Hitler's Germany of a dark-skinned person. On the contrary, watching America's star athlete running and jumping did in fact elicit much admiration and cheers among the spectators, most of whom would not have seen a Negro before. Furthermore, as research revealed, one German sports columnist, describing the athlete's animal-like running and jumping power, daringly called him 'the most popular man of the Games'.

Against the changing face of athletics I remember the pride and joy I felt on being selected to run the second leg in the 4 x 100 m relay at the Milan Championships. Although suffering from the excitement of being abroad for the first time, and the folly of gorging ourselves with juicy grapes and peaches, and other mouth-watering southern fare which had not reached German tables since Hitler came to power, the German team won against strong competition from the Italian, Dutch, Norwegian, Hungarian and Croatian finalists. In 'The Naked Years', I dwelt on the moment the baton was placed into my hand and earlier light rain suddenly turned into a torrential downpour.

> 'I am thrusting myself against the wall of pelting, blinding rain which washes my face, seeps into my mouth, tastes of nothing. The stadium explodes. Cheers are showering the Italian runner in the neighbouring lane, ecstasy is pulling the crowd from their seats, threatening me. And now I am not running for myself, but for Germany, my fatherland; the country of pine forests, Silesian mountains and Rübezahl legend, of Schubert Impromptus, noble Beethoven symphonies and romantic evening songs; the country of Goethe and childhood stories, apple pancakes and *Nusstörtchen*, horse chestnuts and giant sunflowers.'

The rest of my team must have been driven by similar notions, for we established a new European record. We enjoyed our victory for what it meant to each of us. Our leaders, however, would have prized it for the prestige it lent to them individually and to the sports politics of the Reich as a whole.

Then, as during earlier and future events, it was taking part that counted; the honour which such participation bestowed, the satisfaction of having stretched oneself physically and mentally for one's country, home town and team, and this without the dangling carrot of prize money. For me, it was even more: competitive athletics generated and cultivated in me the kind of will power which, like faith, is said to move mountains. Winning was, of course, a most welcome bonus. I would walk taller for days, my head held high and shoulders squared. I was no longer sticking out among my socially more fortunate classmates as one unloved and apparently left by the roadside. Suddenly I was someone to be admired and envied.

Soon, however, the war would be closing in, and athletics, like other sports, had to bow out to 'total war' exigencies. My days as a sprinter and pentathlete were over. So were the years of innocence and ideals. Yet the fighting spirit I acquired on the sports scene would help me in the years to come to cope with the various challenges of my life. It would, ultimately, help me to survive.

2009

'GET SMILEY'

Cold calls, the unsolicited hard-sell landline calls from certain companies to householders of pensionable age, presumed to have disposable income, are the regular curse of my sacred evening leisure.

'I'm calling from...' a trained voice will first ask me to confirm my identity as the householder, before reading off a prepared marketing script. By that time, I either used to hang up or tell the caller in no uncertain terms what I thought of the invasion of my privacy, just when Morse, Barnaby or Hercule Poirot are about to solve some wicked crime. Or when David Attenborough enlightens me on the mating rituals of some rare species.

I should like to know whether any appointments or potential sales are ever made by a cold caller's out-of-hours sales pitch. I also cultivate uncharitable thoughts for those companies and public institutions which, for a fee, supply a list of targetable householders. I don't know why I am one of those singled out. Don't the compilers of such registers realise that I am only a few seasons short of ninety? That I do not need anything but a little comfort, a little love and, by the grace of the weather-god, a little warmth and sunshine? And that, most annoyingly, should I happen to be in another room at the time, I have to move my arthritic frame painfully to the phone? As for my mental state, do companies automatically equate advanced age with gullibility?

The other day I found a temporary antidote to nuisance calls.

'Mrs MacKinnon?' inquired a polite yet authoritative voice. Cautiously, fearful of bad news, I answered in the affirmative.

'Are you the householder?'

Aha, I thought, a cold call. It was time for my own spiel.

182

'No', I said flatly. And with funereal modulation: 'I'm afraid the lady has passed away.'

'Are you the new householder?' queried the caller, implacably.

'No', I replied, 'I'm the cleaner. The house is up for sale.'

The line went dead.

Now, someone might argue that one does not play poker with fate; that by declaring myself 'dead' I was likely to bring about my early departure. But I am not superstitious. I remember my grandmother once receiving a local government letter requesting some details about her recently deceased daughter. My mother, still very much alive at the time, had laughed off her official demise, quoting some German proverb which promises longevity to people mistakenly declared 'dead'. My mother, bless her memory, lived to be ninety-two.

But then, how often can you die on the phone? My next move therefore required a different strategy: I'd forestall the caller's verbal blurb by trumpeting through the line that I did not need a new kitchen, more double glazing or whatever customer-friendly commodity was on offer for a sizeable discount.

Sometimes I might claim that I was on benefit or 'in the red' with my bank; sometimes, acting as if I had expected a call from a friend, I would not allow the caller to get a word in edgeways, by reeling off the latest news about some Helen, Tina or Jean who had at last filed for divorce from her two-timing husband, and - once a free woman - would surely before long tie the knot with some Jack, Dennis or what's his name. It always worked. At least for a time.

However, I soon needed a new ploy. I'd first let the caller get down to business, before breathing suggestively and libidinously down the line. This trick usually throttled the caller and removed my name from the company's list for a few weeks. I doubt, though, that it did much for my reputation.

Now, I won't get quite as rude as a friend of mine who countered the female caller's overture by voicing disgust at her bad breath and recommended a certain toothpaste for halitosis, and a visit to the dentist. 'Before I could mention the benefit of dental floss', my friend said, 'the line went dead.' Perfect.

I won't get that personal. The poor dears detailed by their employers to such boring phoning routine, might be cash-strapped redundant males or single mothers of four living on benefit, working from home.

It now seems that I have run out of strategies. Thus, the next time I am targeted as a potential buyer, I shall not engage in any dialogue, but - uttering a silent expletive - revert to former practice: I shall hang up before the callers have a chance to finish their first sentence. Perhaps, one day, they will get the message.

As it is all too easy nowadays to establish whether a person is alive or dead, too easy to gather details about a subject's financial status or domestic circumstances, I believe that all of us who are victims of cold calls find ourselves in a Catch-22 situation. If any readers know how to kill off such harassing schemes for good, I shall happily recommend them for a knighthood.

And don't tell me that I should register with the Telephone Preference Service. I did several times in the past, but to no avail. I now wonder whether they have a mole among their staff, one who works undercover for certain companies, erasing names of complainants from the TPS register. For a fee, of course.

If such were the case, I'd say: 'GET SMILEY!'[1]

2011

---

[1] London's MI6 senior spy operator during the Cold War, featured in John le Carré's classic novels 'The Spy Who Came In From the Cold', 'Smiley's People' and other East-West spy thrillers.

CLOSE ENCOUNTER

My routine is the same every morning. So is theirs. Come seven o'clock, a blackbird couple - my garden lodgers for many years - will be waiting patiently on the lawn, watching me draw the curtains and serve on the windowsill what in avian circles may rate as a five-star breakfast. Yet, today, our routine was disturbed when a much larger bird with a commanding air appeared and claimed the nutritional fare. And that was not all of it. For, should you be passing my house today, you may be wondering what happened to the pansies in the window-box. I know, they look as if trampled on by a shire horse. Planted lovingly last autumn, and having survived three months of arctic temperatures, snow or fierce winds, their rising sap had just ironed out their leaves, and the first blooms were basking in early spring sunshine, when they got vandalised. The culprit: a male pheasant. Trying in vain to balance himself on the slippery windowsill, he soon found a firmer stance on the flower bed, whence he unashamedly made short shrift of raisins, grapes and other tasty morsels on offer.

What a cheek, I thought. What a beautiful bird!

I was stunned by what I witnessed from behind the window only a foot away. My fearless visitor was, indeed, beautiful, a prize-worthy work of nature. The russet plumage on his back was inlaid with tiny white and gold-coloured, shell-shaped feathers; the white band around his nape brought to mind a Victorian gentleman's stiff, stand-up collar. At the back of the bird's head, hardly visible, tiny erectile crests rose like one of Creation's afterthoughts, while his tail, the best part of two feet long, reminded me of a feather duster. Set into a red patch of feathers, his dark, prominent eyes were constantly on the lookout for whatever might threaten his meal. They also stared at me, the human shape behind the window, which did not move and, ergo, did not ring alarm bells. Now and then, he inspected the row of wooden ducks lined up on the inside windowsill, picking at the glass pane and at what he obviously perceived to be real. When due to his short neck he found himself unable to reach the beak-watering net of nuts hanging on a *Pyracantha* shoot in tantalising proximity, he turned and slowly strode through the window-box, to and fro, like a model on the catwalk, his talons in the process flattening the pansies without compunction.

During the performance he did not waste a single glance on the distraught blackbirds on the lawn, nor on the human spectator. The Stuka-like descent of two feisty male wood pigeons finally called a halt to the show. Belching a *kok-kok*, the pheasant winged himself to the ground and strutted away at a majestic pace.

I am now wondering whether my distinguished visitor will claim priority at the feeding station again. If only the bird weren't so beautiful, so seigneurial, so visibly intelligent and, for me, so privileged a sight to behold at close range, I would chase it away. All I can hope for now is that once he had done what other wild birds will do in spring, he won't be back with his brood.

In the meantime I am not only doing restorative work in the window-box, but I also get up earlier to provide safe breakfast pickings for my blackbirds. Somehow, the couple have caught on and changed their inner feeding clock. And as they respect the new pansy shoots as if they were fledglings, the plants will have a chance to provide a spectacular spring show. I am also delighted to report that my blackbird couple have shown their trust and gratitude by building their nest right next to the kitchen door, well-hidden from predators and not minding the passage of their patron.

As far as my encounter with the noble visitor is concerned, I know I shall never fancy any of his tribe as a paté-ed or roasted gourmet dish - even if he were to return and cause havoc in my window-box again. After all, he's only got a bird's brain.

2010

GAME FOR ONE

Scrabble, the world's leading word game, usually played by two or more players, has long been recognised as a potent mental exercise in that it activates our grey cells and cultivates word-forming skill. It may also be played singly as Scrabble Solitaire. Same number of tiles, same rules, same order of scoring. Yet, as a Solitaire player you have to observe an additional rule: you must not cheat. Honesty is of the essence, even if by a slight manipulation of a word on the board your next move would score double or treble points. What is also different from playing the regular game is that YOU are in sole command. You are the general who deploys his troops and armoury to best advantage, you can speculate, gamble with word computations or use military strategy.

Scrabble Solitaire boasts other welcome advantages: no time limit is set between moves. You may check on what is cooking on the hob, go shopping, have your hair done or e-mail a friend. The board and your waiting tiles are patient. No hassle here, no 'for heaven's sake get on with it' muttered by opponents. Your brain may take a welcome cat-nap or time-out before it musters your tiles again, refreshed and keen.

The game beckons anyone who is in love with language and who enjoys the composition of a drawn set of tiles into a word which, tactically placed, will earn high points. But like its parent game, Scrabble Solitaire may easily become addictive. Such is its lure, such its challenge.

For the Solitaire player the game makes for happy company. It also generates a feel-good factor, most tangibly when landing bumper points or having achieved a high final score. Essentially, though, it is a lone game, lacking the sociable momentum. For in a game for two or more players no limits are set for a laugh, nor for the moans and utterances of frustration when a player's letters turn out to be unplaceable or may earn but pitiful points. And never is a sigh more audible as when - towards the end of the game - the board can no longer offer a vacant place to such maximum value tiles as Q, K or Z.

Played at bedtime, the game has been found by many to have a soporific, rather than a brain-stimulating effect, while insomniacs, often tortured by unwelcome ghosts in the small hours of the night, may find that a few moves on the board will ease them back to bed and into sleep.

With such benefits in mind, Scrabble Solitaire ought to be prescribed by doctors in lieu of tranquillisers and sleeping pills. However, as in bridge, the game's major benefit lies allegedly in its potential to prevent or retard the onset of dementia or Alzheimer's disease. Such findings alone should make the elderly rush to their nearest store and buy a set forthwith to make their grey cells work on a treadmill.

Of no less importance is the fact that the lone player is often steered away from mindless couch-viewing of TV programmes. For this alone, the game surely deserves an extra star. You may ask whether there are any more benefits. Well, yes. Apart from promoting concentration and patience, the game may teach the player gracefully to accept a low final score or a total gridlock. And just as in life, all that is then needed is to clear the board, shuffle the tiles and start again. It is also interesting to note that the highest score obtainable in Scrabble Solitaire remains a mystery.

And now, can you help me make a word from the letters Q R E T U A T. Take as much time as you need.

2011

188

WITH APOLOGIES TO T. S. ELIOT

A Mystery Story

Momentous events are known often to lead to momentous changes. They may radically affect our lifestyle, redefine our philosophy or set new signposts for the future. Then again, it may be no more than a single episode or a string of minor incidents which, as to a drum roll, turn our life around. That is what happened to me.

Mind you, it did start quite dramatically. One morning, thinking of nothing but my first mug of tea, and how best to survive another wild-weather November day, I found a white gold ladies' watch, lavishly encrusted with diamonds, bang in the middle of my living room carpet.

Questions exploded in my mind, stunned my normally placid self. How did it get there overnight? How could it, when I always lock the doors and shut the windows before I retire? And, let's face it, there are no fairy godmothers leaving presents, nor do such exquisite objects fall from the sky like the silver Talers in one of the children's stories by the Brothers Grimm.

Then a thought struck me like a cricket bat. It made my discovery at least feasible, though beyond my rational understanding: The Cat. The Raffles of London. The feline criminal had targeted ME this morning as the receiver of his last night's haul.

I gingerly picked up the watch, which would have had a prime position on a Bond Street jeweller's velvet-covered show tray. Perhaps it had been bought by a wealthy customer for his pampered wife, perhaps for his mistress. And now, like the last pieces of a picture puzzle, things fell into place. Had not the papers been full of what made the nation hold its breath: the exploits of what was believed to be a black tomcat, an assumption based partly on the evidence of an elderly man

189

who, walking home from the pub one night, thought he'd seen an ink-black 'mass' the size of a domestic cat jump over a wall into someone's garden. But he readily admitted that he might have had one pint too many. Yet, in the absence of another explanation, and although hardly plausible, the miscreant was henceforth declared to be a cat.

Quoting T. S. Eliot's popular poem about a mystery cat, which had made into the book The Nation's Hundred Best-loved Poems, a *Times* columnist was quick to refer to the criminal as 'Macavity'. And the name stuck.

According to animal behaviourists, there seemed to be method in the cat's thieving, for Macavity only relieved people of valuables if they were on the Top Rich List, or if they belonged to the celebrity fraternity and were flaunting their new riches like a randy peacock. Not that the master criminal would hoard his loot like a dog a large bone or a squirrel nuts for leaner months. No! The thieving tom would leave saleable items in the homes of pensioners and people living on the breadline. This surely proved - so said the voice of Labour voters - that the cat had a sense of social justice.

Yet the cat burglar was not beyond playing an occasional hoax, the kind which, if word got out - and it always did - was likely to make hilarious pub or dinner conversation. Allegedly, he once left a blue Tory tie on the dresser of an ardent Labour candidate, and a pair of black lace panties where the wife of a two-timing husband could find it. Once a squeaky baby toy ended up in the armchair of a grumpy bachelor and misogynist. Such sporadic tongue-in-cheek deposits, so everyone agreed, showed that the mystery cat had also a sense of humour, surely a freak trait in a domestic animal.

Meanwhile, the police were still out in force and MI5 had started their own investigation after a highly-classified document had disappeared, believed to have been stolen. Surprisingly, it was handed in the following day by an unemployed man of ethnic origin, in the hope that by dint of his honesty he might gain points for his application for British citizenship. Since his English was said to be as good as non-existent, London's spymasters reassured the public that the contents of the document in question were unlikely to have compromised British intelligence.

Yet whatever traps had been set for the villain cum do-gooder, he remained at large, a feline Scarlet Pimpernel who was being 'sought here, there and everywhere'. Scientists were at a loss as to how a cat was able to squeeze through the narrowest of spaces and enjoy a power of levitation which defied the law of gravity. The lack of concrete evidence alone hampered the work of detectives. Forensics, they said, had no more than a paw-print taken at the scene of the burglary, which would obviously be of little use in court, unless the criminal were caught *in flagrante*, and police, lawyers and judges were able to speak in cats' tongues. Anyway, even if caught, the thief would surely produce a cast-iron alibi, just like T. S. Eliot's cat.

The rogue's ill-fame even reached religious services in which Macavity was described as 'a fiend in feline shape'. Cat lovers, though, enthused about 'Moggy's cunning and human-like reasoning', while magicians spoke in awe of his Houdini-like 'artistry'. Soon people were asking 'Where does he get his food from? Where does he sleep? Is he a stray or a cosseted tom whose owners are not aware of his nightly doings?' No wonder that novelists saw in the enigmatic cat the potential for a blockbuster and the annual Mystery Book Award. And while insurers were working overtime, a Macavity look-alike, created by a famous English sculptor from Carrera marble and the size of a Trafalgar Square lion, was drawing crowds to the Tate Modern. Not to be outdone, hobby painters and professional artists were immortalising the cat in watercolour and oil, and a film, entitled With Apologies to T. S. Eliot, starring Colin Firth and Kate Winslet, was showing in London cinemas. An animated version was said to be on the drawing board, 'for the little ones'. Not surprisingly, during one Thursday's televised Prime Minister's Question Time, the feline in question was causing a heated exchange between opposing parties.

I cradled the watch in my hand. I knew I had to take it to the police. Preferably straight away. As a good citizen. But when, in a worsening of the weather, sheets of rain were slapping against the windows and the wind was howling as in a Gothic story, I postponed my errand until the following day.

Well, tomorrow came, and with it another discovery: a single-pearl pendant of rare elegance. Thus, within a week, I became the reluctant recipient of a multi-carat signet ring, a gold bangle, a pair of silver cake tongs, a Roman gold coin, a diamond brooch and, made from alabaster, what looked like the image of a Chinese emperor. It all found a temporary home in one of my drawers, until I could no longer conveniently procrastinate, no longer wait for the right weather, the right hour.

A decision was finally forced upon me, when my mystery donor - perhaps in a facetious mood or having got the address wrong - gifted me with a string-like minuscule 'thing' which I eventually identified as the flimsy 'modesty' cover of young women. Well, that did it. Everything had to go. Today. Now. But would the police believe my story of a fortuitous find? Would I not become the prime suspect in the case, someone aiding and abetting? Surely I would be endlessly questioned; detectives would search my house and guard the premises, perhaps staying overnight in shifts? Some people might even speculate, whisper that I might have been working hand-in-paw with the law-breaker. Others might speak behind my back of a lonely widow trying to garner some excitement or hoping to sell her story for a multi-figure sum. Yet I was intrigued. Why had the cat presented me lately with other people's valuables? Did he know that I was struggling with my bills? Charitable thoughts, though hardly imaginable, might well have been behind the reason for his stunts, I mused, but a cat, even of Macavity's intelligence, would have no knowledge of the human interpretation of right and wrong, as anchored in the Bible's Ten Commandments and in the Law, nor would he realise that the stolen items would be considered 'hot' property, unsaleable by every reputable jeweller, antiquarian and auctioneer.

Braving the kind of weather in which dogs and cats refuse to go out and every non-essential errand is postponed, I presented myself at the local police station.

'This is what I found in the park this morning', I said, explaining that come rain or shine I always go for a walk after breakfast. 'Awful weather though', I added. 'I nearly changed my mind.' I heaved my holdall onto the sergeant's desk. 'It looks as if it is part of the stolen goods everybody is reading about.' The contents gleamed in the strong overhead light, and I thought the officer looked like Kafka's Gregor Samsa when, on waking, he found himself metamorphosed into a beetle. Once the sergeant had collected himself, he took my name and address and, rolling out the red carpet, took me to see his superior officer. I repeated my story and soon sunned myself in the glow of his official delight and personal admiration for what he called 'an honest citizen of the old school'.

'Funny you spotting what a team of constables and detectives have failed to locate for weeks', he said. 'There is a handsome reward, of course, and I wouldn't be surprised if you were to receive an invitation to Buckingham Palace'.

'Oh, please', I countered, 'no fuss. I like to remain anonymous. Mind you, a little money wouldn't come amiss. My boiler... and there's a leak in the roof...'

A police car took me home. As it was still too early for lunch, I made myself a cup of coffee and, armed with the day's crossword, went to sit in my armchair. That was when I saw it: a black tomcat with white paws, curled up behind the cushion.

'Hello, Macavity!' I said, once I had found my voice. 'I may take it you are the mystery cat, the master criminal. Eh?'

The cat remained inert. Eyes the colour of a sunlit lagoon looked at me. And now, with all the *sang froid* I could muster, I established who was the mistress of the house.

'Look here', I said, wiggling my forefinger, 'this is MY chair. You may lie on the sofa. Alright?' With wary hands and a honey-dripping voice I shifted the bundle, meeting with no resistance during such a venture, nor any scratching, teeth-baring or angry hissing. Surely, I thought, an unusual behaviour for a tomcat, and something for the cat-lovers' history book. The 'most-wanted' criminal soon nestled himself back into a sleeping and watching position, and this on *my* settee, in *my* house!

Lunch that day was for two.

My visitor was licking his paws when I delivered my homily. 'Listen', I said, 'as from now your name will be 'Blackie'. And if you want to use my house as a safe-house and be my lodger, you'll have to abide by my rules. Now, first of all, there will be no more thieving. You will also not bring in dead mice, and you will allow my songbirds to enjoy a long life. And if you have to do what other toms do, you'll make sure that you and your tribe do not wake up the whole neighbourhood. In return, I shall buy you food and treats and a red collar with a little bell. Also, first thing tomorrow morning, I'll take you to the vet for a health check. You know - worms, fleas, bugs, the usual routine. After all, my dear, you've been around, as they say. Only then can you have the freedom of my house. But I repeat: no more pilfering. Agreed?'

Blackie's excited tail seemed to seal our contract.

That afternoon, in the garden, with the cat sniffing new territory, my neighbour - known for her unhealthy probing into other people's affairs - called me over to the fence.

'I see you've got yourself a cat', she said. 'A tomcat. Where did you find him? He looks like the cat they call 'Macavity'.'

'Oh no', I replied. 'Blackie is my daughter's. She and her family are moving to Australia. She did not want him to go to a cattery. Isn't he lovely?'

Back in the house, back in my armchair, I felt a paw on my knee, and sensed my new companion's wish to sit on my lap. Whiskers, a soft nose, brushed my cheek. An affection-seeking tomcat? Surely this was the stuff of which cat stories are made.

A week passed. There came no further reports of the mysterious thieving and redistribution of objects. Readers looked in vain for the 'Macavity' column in their newspapers, which noted a marked drop in sales. Some people suggested that the cat had retired; others spoke of how easily a prowling feline can be run over by a drink-driver at night. A Eurotunnel customs officer admitted that their checks were not always foolproof, and that the criminal might have fled, or have relocated, to France. One worried reader reported that they'd seen a Chinese restaurant chef grinning and smacking his lips at the mention of the cat.

Strangely enough, the news of the recovered valuables, which police were holding in safe custody pending the identification of their owners, caused only a flash of interest. Blackie, alias Macavity, had become yesterday's news. He would resurface in time at Madame Tussauds and live on in school children's ditties about a cat called Macavity.

What, I often mused, if people knew that the former master criminal and I were enjoying a happy *ménage à deux*? What if T. S. Eliot were to know how his poem could have ended?

2011

195

Text transcribed by Black Cat Secretarial Services
01843 295264
www.writeserve.com